# THE
# EVERYTHING

# MOTHER GOOSE
# BOOK

## 300 favorites kids will enjoy, again and again

Edited By
June Rifkin

Adams Media Corporation
Holbrook, Massachusetts

An Everything® Series Book. The Everything® Series is a
registered trademark of Adams Media Corporation.

Published by Adams Media Corporation
260 Center Street, Holbrook, MA 02343 U. S. A.
www.adamsmedia.com

ISBN: 1-58062-490-1

Printed in the United States of America.

J  I  H  G  F  E  D  C  B  A


**Library of Congress Cataloging-in-Publication Data**
The everything mother goose book / [collected by] June Rifkin.
p.        cm.
Summary: A collection of nearly 300 nursery rhymes accompanied by
a section with background and suggestions for using the rhymes.
ISBN 1-58062-490-1
1. Nursery rhymes. 2. Children's poetry. [1. Nursery rhymes.] I. Rifkin, June.
PZ8.3 .E97          2001
398.8--dc21          00-066349

Illustrations by Barry Littmann

*This book is available at quantity discounts for bulk purchases.*
*For information, call 1-800-872-5627.*

**Visit the entire Everything® series at everything.com**

## Dedication

It's a pleasure to share this book with all the "little ones" in my
life who will grow up with and enjoy this book:

Madison Faith and Jordyn Kari Rifkin
Bobbi November and Sonny November Rifkin
McKenzie Taylor Clark
Jonah Paul Clark
Alexander Bates Koffman
And, even the "big ones" too, most importantly,
my son, Colin Spencer.

# Acknowledgments

A big "thanks" to my editor, Pam Liflander, for the IOU.
And to Chris Harris for providing me
with historical tidbits from England.

# Contents

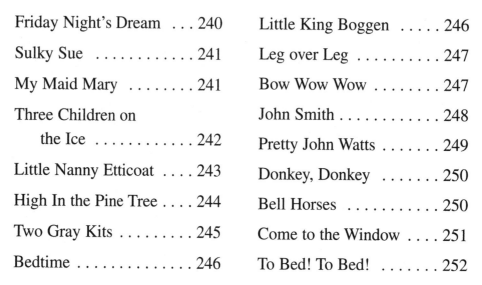

# Introduction

## Lives Touched by Rhymes

At the age of five, I made my stage debut at the Bee Hive Nursery School in Flushing, New York, as none other than Little Bo Peep. Garbed in a gingham dress and a white pinafore and holding a herding staff, I stood on stage among the cardboard and cotton sheep, rubbing my eyes to feign a cry . . . until I caught a glimpse of my doting mother and grandmother in the audience. At that point, I cracked a small smile, which was instantly captured on film by the professional photographer hired for the day. Upon gazing at this faded color photo thirty years later, my then four-year-old son, Colin, remarked, "Why are you smiling? Isn't Little Bo Peep supposed to be sad because she lost her sheep!"

"Well," I explained, "the photo was taken *after* the sheep came home."

Choosing to play Little Bo Peep on "Nursery Rhyme Day" at school was an easy decision. The character and her plight were ingrained in my memory from the picture books I read with my mom and from a little yellow plastic 78 rpm record filled with rhymes set to music that I played over and over again on my kiddie record player. Most of all, I remember how every Thanksgiving Day throughout my childhood, my grandfather and I would watch the annual telecast of a Laurel and Hardy movie called *March of the Wooden Soldiers*. The movie, which took a humorous spin on the Victor Herbert operetta, *Babes in Toyland*, revolves around how Little Bo Peep is forced into marriage with an ugly villain named Barnaby, even though she is in love with Tom the Piper's Son. All the famous

nursery rhyme characters appear in the film, and when Bo loses her sheep, everyone helps her look for them. Comic intervention ensues with Stan Laurel's character, in full bridal drag, standing in for Bo Peep at the dreaded wedding and, of course, everyone living happily ever after, including Bo and Tom, who reunite in the end. So, you could say that during my preschool years, I had a true affinity to nursery rhymes and, in particular, to Little Bo Peep and her sheep. It's also no surprise that I've never been able to eat lamb!

It's hard to imagine a life without nursery rhymes. Most of our earliest memories are of parents, grandparents, or other loved ones reading or reciting rhymes to us while sitting in their laps. How many times can you recall playing and singing "See-Saw" and getting dipped upside down and pulled up again and again with every line until dizzy with giggles? Or having "This Little Piggy" acted out on your toes, and getting tickled from foot to neck as the last little piggy went "wee, wee, wee, all the way home?" Or using "Eenie, Meeny, Miney, Mo" to choose who goes first in a game? Rhymes and their accompanying tunes or games are the common threads that connect us as children.

As adults, we instinctively lapse into reciting and playing those same rhymes and games with our own children, nieces and nephews, or grandchildren. "Pat-A-Cake" . . . "Ring a Ring O' Roses" . . . "See-Saw" . . . these rhymes are as integral to childhood as teddy bears, nightlights, and "blankies."

In *The Everything® Mother Goose Book*, you'll have an opportunity to share many of your favorite or long forgotten rhymes with that special child—or children—in your life. You might even learn new rhymes, too. Most of all, everyone will have hours of fun together creating new memories to last a lifetime.

—June Rifkin
Riverdale, New York

# Rhymes and Reasons

Why do nursery rhymes continue to be popular with children and their parents generation after generation? Simple. They're easy to remember, fun to recite, and filled with colorful images about good or naughty boys and girls, kings and queens and other royalty, cute little animals, quirky characters of both genders, and quaint little towns. Rhymes are a delight with children whether it's playtime, bedtime, or passing the time away.

Psychologists and educators believe that introducing children to nursery rhymes at an early age encourages auditory and speech development, promotes reading skills, and fosters concentration. Rhymes take many forms. There are counting rhymes like "1, 2, Buckle My Shoe," and tongue-twisters like "Peter Piper picked a peck of pickled peppers." There are also lullabies ("Rock-a-bye baby, on the treetop"), hand-play ("Pat-a-Cake"), and dances ("Here we go round the mulberry bush").

Nursery rhymes are popularized on records, home videos, interactive toys and software, and on TV shows. Children's "characters" and mainstream performers continue to embrace and entertain with rhymes. TV's big purple dinosaur, Barney, incorporates rhymes into his show; children's entertainment trio, Sharon, Lois, and Bram sing many well-know rhyme songs in their stage and TV performances; Grammy and Oscar-winning singer-songwriter, Carly Simon integrated "Itsy Bitsy Spider" into her hit song "Coming Around Again"; and even comedian Andrew Dice Clay gave a crude and immoral spin to notable rhymes like "Jack and Jill" and "Little Miss Muffet" in his standup comedy act.

Filled with characters whose names and images are as familiar to us as family members—Old King Cole, Miss Muffet, Jack Sprat, and even the Three Blind Mice—there seems no doubt that these memorable and beloved verses will remain a part of Western culture for many centuries to come.

## A Brief History of Nursery Rhymes

Nursery rhymes have been around for centuries, originating as early as the 15th century. Until the first collection of rhymes appeared in print in the 18th century, rhymes were passed along orally from generation to generation. Each culture has its own variations and claims to origin. Many originated from politics or historical events, or were based on the lives or actions of real people. Some were adapted from ballads, plays, merchant cries, or proverbs. And others were created to entertain or educate children, or to soothe fussy babies to sleep in the form of lullabies. It seems likely, however, that the majority of early rhymes were created for the benefit of adults rather than children. Sometimes, we become so swept up in the delightful, rhythmic meter of reciting the verses that we barely take notice of the sometimes dark, mature, or bawdy nature of the rhyme itself.

One of the earliest collection of rhymes was contained in a tiny-sized book in two volumes called *Tommy Thumb's Pretty Song Book*, published in England in 1744. Around 1781, another collection of rhymes, *Mother Goose's Melody (or Sonnets for the Cradle)*, was published by John Newbery, who became noted for children's books in England and whose name is familiar to us today from the famed Newbery Award for children's literature. *Mother Goose's Melody* was reprinted in America in 1786 by pub-

lisher Isaiah Thomas (no relation to the former Detroit Piston). Which now brings us to ask the question . . .

## Who Is Mother Goose?

Most people, particularly Americans, equate nursery rhymes with Mother Goose, especially since her name and image is usually prevalent on books, recordings, or film/TV/videos related to nursery rhymes. But is Mother Goose real?

There is much speculation on the origins of Mother Goose with little confirmation as to her true identity or existence. When she's not characterized as a goose with granny glasses and a bonnet, she is usually depicted as an old woman, either a homely but doting caricature, or as a more magical presence, donning a tall hat and riding a goose. If she was, indeed, a real person, it is unlikely she resembled either. Some scholars believe she was Bertrada of Laon, the mother of the medieval French ruler, Charlemagne. Queen Bertrada was affectionately called Queen Goosefoot, hence "Mother Goose." Others suggest that she is Elizabeth Goose (or Vergoose or Vertigoose), a beloved mother and grandmother who regaled children with stories and rhymes in Colonial Boston. Allegedly, her son-in-law Thomas Fleet, who was a printer, published a compilation of her verses called *Songs for the Nursery or Mother Goose's Melodies for Children,* though no copy of this book has ever been found. Oddly enough, this legend is perpetuated through a tombstone located at the Granary Burying Ground in Boston, Massachusetts. The inscription on the tombstone refers to a "Mary Goose," wife of Isaac Goose

(Elizabeth's husband), but no one knows if there is even a body buried beneath this stone and, if so, if it belongs to Elizabeth Goose. Still, the grave seems to attract tourists and nursery-rhyme fans from around the world.

In 1697, a French writer named Charles Perrault published a book of popular fairy tales that included "Cinderella" and "Little Red Riding Hood," called *Histoires ou Contes du temps passe* (roughly translated as *Tales of Past Times*). The cover contained the phrase *Contes de Ma Mere L'Oye,* which translated into English is "Tales of Mother Goose." The book was translated and published in London retaining the same art and titles. Many believe, this is indeed the origin of Mother Goose. Whatever the case may be, by the time *Mother Goose's Melody* was published in England and soon after in America, nursery rhymes and the name "Mother Goose" would forever be associated.

At the end of the day, whether or not she ever existed seems irrelevant. Mother Goose was, is, and will forever be a symbol of classic, important, and influential literature and oral tradition that enlightens and touches the souls of everyone.

## Origins of Nursery Rhymes

The origins of nursery rhymes are as vague and debated as the origins of Mother Goose. Since many rhymes were based on songs, stories, or historical events and then passed on orally long before they were documented, there is much speculation over what events or people certain

rhymes are based. The rhymes of yesteryear were the equivalent of today's tabloid press, with people spreading the news by passing along sensational stories in the form of verse. As with any form of oral communication, something inevitably gets lost or misconstrued in the translation. Truth, half-truth, or mere fabrication, some of the alleged backgrounds are interesting and intriguing.

Here's a quick glimpse into some possible origins of popular rhymes:

## Humpty Dumpty

Humpty Dumpty sat on a wall,
Humpty Dumpty had a great fall.
All the King's horses and all the King's men,
Couldn't put Humpty together again.

Though in modern times he is portrayed as an egg, according to some English historians, Humpty Dumpty was a cannon aimed against Parliamentary troops during a siege at a Royalist castle during a civil war. But disaster struck when the cannon, which was mounted on a wall, fell and broke into several pieces ("All the King's horses and all the King's men, couldn't put Humpty together again").

It is also speculated that Humpty Dumpty is really King Richard III of England.

# Ring a Ring O' Roses

A popular circle game with children, the 21st-century version of the rhyme goes:

Ring around the rosy
A pocket full of posies,
Ashes, ashes,
We all fall down!

However, earlier versions (namely British) offer a slight variation:

Ring a ring of roses
A pocket full of posies,
A-tishoo, a-tishoo
We all fall down!

Allegedly, this rhyme is about the Great Plague. The "ring a ring of roses" refers to the rash the illness forms on the skin; "posies" were the flowers that people carried to ward off the infection (or else were used on the dead bodies to hide the stench); "a-tishoo, a-tishoo" was the violent sneezing associated with the final symptoms of the illness; and of course, "we all fall down," means final death.

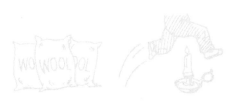

## Little Jack Horner

Little Jack Horner
Sat in the corner,
Eating a Christmas pie:
He put in his thumb,
And pulled out a plum,
And said, "What a good boy am I!"

Legend has it that when Henry VIII of England ordered the dissolution of the monasteries, property deeds were sent to the King concealed in a pie. One of these deeds made its way to Thomas Horner, a supporter of the King. Whether he bought the property outright, was given it by the King, or acquired the property through direct contact with the infamous pie is up for debate. However, there is documentation to support that Horner did indeed acquire former church property. Regardless of how, it was a "plum," indeed.

## Hot Cross Buns

Hot cross buns!
Hot cross buns!
One a penny, two a penny,
Hot cross buns!

If you have no daughters,
Give them to your sons.
One a penny, two a penny,
Hot cross buns!

This rhyme has its origins from cries sung by vendors selling their wares in street markets.

## Goosey, Goosey, Gander

Goosey, goosey, gander,
Where shall I wander?
Upstairs and downstairs
And in my lady's chamber.

There I met an old man
Who wouldn't say his prayers;
I took him by the left leg,
And threw him down the stairs.

An interesting story places this rhyme back again during the reign of King Henry VIII. Henry's fifth wife (of eight!), Catherine Howard, was a young and beautiful woman with many admirers. Highly promiscuous, Catherine had several affairs under the King's nose—hence, "upstairs and downstairs and in my lady's chamber." Upon Henry's discovery of these indiscretions, he had Catherine and her paramours beheaded—a slightly more aggressive and permanent revenge than simply throwing them "down the stairs."

# Fun with Rhymes

With 300 rhymes at your fingertips, there are many ways you and your children (or anyone who's young at heart) can enhance the enjoyment of these beloved little ditties.

## Party Time

Host a nursery-rhyme theme party for your toddler or preschooler. Guests can dress up as their favorite rhyme characters and recite the rhyme (by heart or with the help of a parent or friend). You can decorate with rhyme-theme items and even serve dishes based on nursery rhymes (see recipe suggestions following for more details).

## School/Day Care Play

If you're a teacher or day care provider, a nursery-rhyme show can be lots of fun for the kids (or, if you're a parent, suggest the idea to your child's teacher). Children can dress up as nursery-rhyme characters and recite the rhymes on stage. If the children are very young, they can come to the stage in costume and you can play recordings of the songs or spoken verses for each rhyme.

The children will also enjoy painting sets for the show or creating props, like sheep made of cotton!

## Arts and Crafts

Have children create their own nursery-rhyme books that highlight their favorite rhymes. They can make their own illustrations with crayons, markers, or colored pencils. Paste on feathers for the birds, cotton on the pussycats, or glitter on the crowns of kings and queens.

## Car Games

Car trips can be dull, especially if you have a long drive or get stuck in traffic. Why not amuse your children—and yourself—by making up some fun guessing games or trivia questions using the rhymes? Here are some questions to start with that will get everyone thinking:

1. How many nursery rhymes can you think of that have a character named "Jack" (or "Tom" or "Mary" or "Peter")?
2. Name all the rhymes you know that are about an "old woman" (or an "old man").
3. Which rhymes feature kings or queens?
4. How many rhymes can you think of that feature cats (or birds)?
5. What cities or towns are featured in some rhymes?
6. Jack Sprat could eat no fat. What couldn't his wife eat?
7. What fruit did Jack Horner pull out of the pie with his thumb?
8. How many were "going to St. Ives?" (Bonus: Where is St. Ives?)
9. What kind of animal was Dapple-Gray?
10. Can you name all the churches mentioned in "The Bells of St. Helen's?"

Another way to pass the time is with a "Sing-A-Long." Lots of rhymes have accompanying tunes, so introduce your children to the songs if they don't already know them. And, if they do, start singing! You might get stares from people in the cars next to you—if so, roll down the window and have them join in!

## Spot the Rhyme Character

Whenever you're stuck somewhere—in a long line, at the doctor's office, at an airport, etc.—have some wicked fun with your family by looking around you and seeing if you can find people who look like famous rhyme characters. Can you find the "little girl with the curl?" How about someone who looks like Mother Goose? Or Humpty Dumpty? (Be polite—make sure the kids don't point fingers!)

## Recipe Ideas from Mother Goose's Kitchen

If you're having a kids' party or just want something fun to do on a rainy day, create a meal with dishes selected from favorite nursery rhymes.

- Miss Muffet's Curds and Whey (Cottage Cheese)
- Hot Pease Porridge (Oatmeal)
- Curly Locks' Strawberry, Sugar, and Cream
- Georgie Porgie's Pudding and Pie
- Hot Cross Buns
- Jack Horner's Christmas Pie (with plums)
- Tommy Tucker's White Bread and Butter

- Peter Pumpkin Eater's Pumpkin Pie
- Pussycat's Dumplings
- The Queen of Heart's Summer Tarts
- This Little Piggy's Roast Beef

## Nursery Rhyme Fun on Home Video

The following is a list of Mother Goose-related videos/DVDs the whole family can enjoy:

- *March of the Wooden Soldiers* (1934)
  The wonderful Laurel and Hardy classic colorized and available on VHS and DVD.
- *Mother Goose Rock 'N Rhyme* (1990)
  Entertaining musical starring Shelley Duvall, Little Richard, Cyndi Lauper, Paul Simon, Woody Harrelson, and Garry Shandling.
- *Babes in Toyland* (1961)
  Classic Walt Disney musical starring Annette Funicello, Tommy Sands, and Ray Bolger.
- *Barney Rhymes with Mother Goose* (1993)
  Barney the Dinosaur and friends help Mother Goose with her rhymes.
- *Happily Ever After: Fairy Tales for Every Child—Mother Goose: A Rappin' and a Rhymin' Fairy Tale* (1997)
  Animated feature with the voices of Whoopi Goldberg, Salt-N-Pepa, Jimmy Smits, Denzel Washington, and Robert Guillaume.
- *William Wegman's Mother Goose* (1997)
  Wegman's famous Weimaraners are dressed up as various nursery rhyme characters to teach kids rhymes.

# Nursery Rhymes

# Mary Had a Little Lamb

Mary had a little lamb
Its fleece was white as snow,
And everywhere that Mary went
The lamb was sure to go.

He followed her to school one day
Which was against the rule
It made the children laugh and play
To see a lamb at school.

And so the teacher turned him out,
But still he lingered near,
And waited patiently about
Till Mary did appear.

"What makes the lamb love Mary so?"
The eager children cry.
"Why, Mary loves the lamb, you know,"
The teacher did reply.

# Three Blind Mice

Three blind mice! See how they run!
They all ran after the farmer's wife,
Who cut off their tails with a carving knife.
Did you ever see such a thing in your life
As three blind mice?

# This Little Pig

This little pig went to market;

This little pig stayed at home;

This little pig had roast beef;

This little pig had none;

This little pig cried, "Wee, wee, wee!"

All the way home.

# Little Miss Muffet

Little Miss Muffet
Sat on a tuffet,
Eating of curds and whey;
Along came a big spider,
And sat down beside her,
And frightened
Miss Muffet away.

# Hickory, Dickory, Dock

Hickory, dickory, dock!
The mouse ran up the clock;
The clock struck one,
And down he run,
Hickory, dickory, dock!

# Baa, Baa, Black Sheep

Baa, baa, black sheep,
Have you any wool?
Yes, sir, yes, sir,
Three bags full:
One for my master,
One for my dame,
And one for the little boy
Who lives in the lane.

# To Market, to Market

To market, to market, to buy a fat pig,

Home again, home again, jiggety jig.

To market, to market, to buy a fat hog,

Home again, home again, jiggety jog.

To market, to market, to buy a plum bun,

Home again, home again, market is done.

# Old Woman, Old Woman

There was an old woman tossed in a basket.
Seventeen times as high as the moon;
But where she was going no mortal could tell,
For under her arm she carried a broom.

"Old woman, old woman, old woman," said I,
"Whither, oh whither, oh whither so high?"
"To sweep the cobwebs from the sky;
And I'll be with you by-and-by."

# Cocks Crow
# in the Morn

Cocks crow in the morn
To tell us to rise,
And he who lies late
Will never be wise;
For early to bed
And early to rise,
Is the way to be healthy
And wealthy and wise.

# Old Mother Hubbard

Old Mother Hubbard
Went to the cupboard,
To give her poor dog a bone;
But when she got there
The cupboard was bare,
And so the poor dog
    had none.

She took a clean dish
To get him some tripe,
But when she came back
He was smoking a pipe.
She went to the grocer's
To buy him some fruit,
But when she came back
He was playing the flute.

She went to the baker's
To buy him some bread,
But when she came back
The poor dog was dead.
She went to the undertaker's
To buy him a coffin,

But when she came back
The poor dog was laughing.

She went to the hatter's
To buy him a hat,
But when she came back
He was feeding the cat.

The dame made a curtsey,
The dog made a bow,
The dame said, "Your servant."
The dog said, "Bow wow!"

# The Queen of Hearts

The Queen of Hearts,
She made some tarts,
All on a summer's day;
The Knave of Hearts,
He stole the tarts,
  And took them clean away.

  The King of Hearts
    Called for the tarts,
      And beat the Knave full sore;
      The Knave of Hearts
        Brought back the tarts,
          And vowed he'd steal no more.

# Twinkle, Twinkle, Little Star

Twinkle, twinkle, little star,

How I wonder what you are.

Up above the world so high,

Like a diamond in the sky.

Twinkle, twinkle, little star,

How I wonder what you are.

# Solomon Grundy

Solomon Grundy,
Born on a Monday,
Christened on Tuesday,
Married on Wednesday,
Took ill on Thursday,
Worse on Friday,
Died on Saturday,
Buried on Sunday.
This is the end
Of Solomon Grundy.

# Old Chairs to Mend

If I'd as much money as I could spend,
I never would cry old chairs to mend;
Old chairs to mend, old chairs to mend;
I never would cry old chairs to mend.

If I'd as much money as I could tell,
I never would cry old clothes to sell;
Old clothes to sell, old clothes to sell;
I never would cry old clothes to sell.

# Hark! Hark!

Hark! Hark! The dogs do bark!
Beggars are coming to town:
Some in jags, and some in rags
And some in velvet gown.

# Where Has My Little Dog Gone?

Oh where, oh where has my little dog gone?
Oh where, oh where can he be?
With his ears cut short and his tail cut long,
Oh where, oh where can he be?

# A Swarm of Bees in May

A swarm of bees in May
Is worth a load of hay;
A swarm of bees in June
Is worth a silver spoon;
A swarm of bees in July
Is not worth a fly.

# Simple Simon

Simple Simon met a pieman,
Going to the fair;
Says Simple Simon to the pieman,
"Let me taste your ware."

Says the pieman to Simple Simon,
"Show me first your penny."
Says Simple Simon to the pieman,
"Indeed, I have not any."

# Oh, Dear, What Can the Matter Be?

Oh, dear, what can the matter be?
Oh, dear, what can the matter be?
Oh, dear, what can the matter be?
Johnny's so long at the fair.

He promised he'd buy me a
    bunch of blue ribbons,
He promised he'd buy me a
    bunch of blue ribbons,
He promised he'd buy me a
    bunch of blue ribbons,
To tie up my bonny
    brown hair.

# Mary, Mary, Quite Contrary

Mary, Mary, quite contrary,
How does your garden grow?
Silver bells and cockle shells,
And pretty maids all of a row.

# The Seasons

Spring is showery, flowery, bowery;
Summer—hoppy, croppy, poppy;
Autumn—wheezy, sneezy, freezy;
Winter—slippy, drippy, nippy.

# Dapple–Gray

I had a little pony,
His name was Dapple–Gray,
I lent him to a lady,
To ride a mile away.
She whipped him, she slashed him,
She rode him through the mire;
I would not lend my pony now
For all the lady's hire.

# The Itsy Bitsy Spider

The itsy bitsy spider climbed up the water spout,
Down came the rain and washed the spider out.
Out came the sun and dried up all the rain,
And the itsy bitsy spider climbed up the
    spout again.

# Little Bobby Snooks

Little Bobby Snooks was fond of his books,
And loved by his usher and master;
But naughty Jack Spry, he got a black eye,
And carries his nose in a plaster.

# Robin Redbreast

Little Robin Redbreast sat upon a tree,
Up went Pussycat, down went he,
Down came Pussycat, away Robin ran,
Says little Robin Redbreast: "Catch me if you can!"

Little Robin Redbreast jumped
    upon a spade,
    Pussycat jumped after him, and
    then he was afraid.
Little Robin chirped and sang,
    and what did Pussy say?
Pussycat said: "Mew, mew,
    mew," and Robin flew away.

# Peter Piper

Peter Piper picked a peck of pickled peppers;

A peck of pickled peppers Peter Piper picked.

If Peter Piper picked a peck of pickled peppers,

Where's the peck of pickled peppers Peter Piper picked?

# Cushy Cow

Cushy cow, bonny, let down thy milk,
And I will give thee a gown of silk;
A gown of silk and a silver tee,
If thou wilt let down thy milk to me.

# This Is the Way the Ladies Ride

This is the way the ladies ride,
Tri, tre, tre, tree,
Tri, tre, tre, tree!
This is the way the ladies ride,
Tri, tre, tre, tre
Tri tre tre–tree!

This is the way the gentlemen ride,
Gallop–a–trot,
Gallop–a–trot!
This is the way the gentlemen ride,
Gallop–a–gallop–a–trot!

This is the way the farmers ride,
Hobbledy–hoy,
Hobbledy–hoy!
This is the way the farmers ride,
Hobbledy–hobbledy–hoy!

# Ring a Ring O' Roses

Ring a ring o' roses,
A pocketful of posies.
Ashes, ashes,
We all fall down.

# Around the Green Gravel

Around the green gravel the grass grows green,
And all the pretty maids are plain to be seen;
Wash them with milk, and clothe them with silk,
And write their names with a pen and ink.

# See–Saw

See–saw, Margery Daw,
Jackie shall have a new master.
He shall have but a penny a day
Because he can work no faster.

# See Saw, Sacradown

See, saw, sacradown
What is the way to London town?
One foot up, the other foot down,
That is the way to London town.

# Lucy Locket

Lucy Locket lost her pocket,
Kitty Fisher found it;
There was not a penny in it
But a ribbon around it.

# A Ten O'Clock Scholar

A diller, a dollar, a ten o'clock scholar—
What makes you come so soon?
You used to come at ten o'clock,
But now you come at noon.

# Polly Put the Kettle On

Polly, put the kettle on,
Polly, put the kettle on,
Polly, put the kettle on,
We'll all have tea.

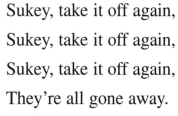

Sukey, take it off again,
Sukey, take it off again,
Sukey, take it off again,
They're all gone away.

# Three Little Kittens

Three little kittens,
They lost their mittens,
And they began to cry,
"Oh, mother dear, we sadly fear
Our mittens we have lost."

"What! Lost your mittens,
You silly kittens!
Then you shall have no pie.
Mee–ow, mee–ow, mee–ow.
No, you shall have no pie."

The three little kittens,
They found their mittens,
And they began to cry,
"Oh, mother dear, see here, see here,
Our mittens we have found."

"Put on your mittens,
You happy kittens,
And you shall have some pie,
Purr–r, purr–r, purr–r,
Oh, let us have some pie."

The three little kittens
Put on their mittens,
And soon ate up the pie;
"Oh, mother dear, we greatly fear
Our mittens we have soiled."

"What! Soiled your mittens,
You silly kittens!"
Then they began to sigh,
"Mee–ow, mee–ow, mee–ow."
Then they began to sigh.

The three little kittens,
They washed their mittens,
And hung them out to dry;
"Oh, mother dear, do you not hear
Our mittens we have washed?"

"What! Washed your mittens,
Then you're good kittens!
Now it's time for bed, bye–bye.
Purr–r, Purr–r, Purr–r,
It's time for bed, bye–bye."

# Rock-a-Bye Baby

Rock–a–bye baby, on the tree top,

When the wind blows the cradle will rock;

When the bough breaks the cradle will fall;

And down will come baby, cradle and all.

# Bye, Baby Bunting

Bye, baby bunting,

Daddy's gone a–hunting,

To get a little rabbit skin,

To wrap the baby bunting in.

# I Saw a Ship A–Sailing

I saw a ship a–sailing,
A–sailing on the sea,
And, oh, it was all laden
With pretty things for thee.

There were comfits in the cabin,
And apples in the hold,
The sails were made of silk,
And the masts were made of gold.

The four–and–twenty sailors
That stood between the decks,
Were four–and–twenty white mice
With chains about their necks.

The captain was a duck,
With a packet on his back;
And when the ship began to move,
The captain said, "Quack! Quack!"

# There Was a Crooked Man

There was a crooked man, and he went a crooked mile,
He found a crooked sixpence against a crooked stile;
He bought a crooked cat, which caught a crooked mouse,
And they all lived together in a little crooked house.

# As I Went Through the Garden Gap

As I went through the garden gap,
Who should I meet but Dick Redcap!
A stick in his hand, a stone in his throat,
If you'll tell me this riddle, I'll give you
    a groat.

# A Duck and a Drake

A duck and a drake,

And a halfpenny cake,

With a penny to pay the old baker.

A hop and a scotch

Is another notch,

Slitherum, slatherum, take her.

# Jack and Jill

Jack and Jill went up the hill,
To fetch a pail of water;
Jack fell down, and broke his crown,
And Jill came tumbling after.

Up Jack got and home did trot,
As fast as he could caper,
Went to bed and plastered his head
With vinegar and brown paper.

# The Little Girl with a Curl

There was a little girl who had a little curl
Right in the middle of her forehead;
When she was good, she was very, very good,
And when she was bad she was horrid.

# Hush Baby Dolly

Hush, baby, my dolly, I pray you don't cry,
And I'll give you some bread, and some milk
　　by–and–by;
Or perhaps you like custard, or, maybe, a tart,
Then to either you're welcome, with all my heart.

# Lavender Blue

Lavender blue and rosemary green,
When I am king you shall be queen;
Call up my maids at four o'clock,
Some to the wheel and some to the rock;
Some to make hay and some to shear corn,
And you and I will keep the bed warm.

# Christmas Is Coming

Christmas is coming, the geese are getting fat,
Please to put a penny in an old man's hat;
If you haven't got a penny, a halfpenny will do,
If you haven't got a halfpenny, God bless you.

# The Cats Went Out to Serenade

The cats went out to serenade
And on a banjo sweetly played;
And summer nights they climbed a tree
And sand, "My love, oh, come to me!"

# Eenie, Meeny, Miney, Mo

Eenie, meeny, miney, mo
Catch a tiger by the toe,
If he hollers, let him go
Eenie, meeny, miney, mo.

# If

If all the world were apple pie,
And all the sea were ink,
And all the trees were bread and cheese,
What should we have for drink?

# What Are Little Boys Made Of?

What are little boys made of?
What are little boys made of?
"Snaps and snails, and puppy–dogs' tails;
And that's what little boys are made of."

What are little girls made of?
What are little girls made of?
"Sugar and spice, and all that's nice;
And that's what little girls are made of."

# The Dusty Miller

Margaret wrote a letter,
Sealed it with her finger,
Threw it in the dam
For the dusty miller.
Dusty was his coat,
Dusty was the silver,
Dusty was the kiss
I'd from the dusty miller.
If I had my pockets
Full of gold and silver,
I would give it all
To my dusty miller.

# How Many Days Has My Baby to Play?

How many days has my baby to play?
Saturday, Sunday, Monday,
Tuesday, Wednesday, Thursday, Friday,
Saturday, Sunday, Monday.

# When Papa Comes Home

You shall have an apple,
You shall have a plum,
You shall have a rattle,
When papa comes home.

# Coffee and Tea

Molly, my sister, and I fell out,
And what do you think it was all about?
She loved coffee and I loved tea,
And that was the reason we couldn't agree.

# Elizabeth, Elspeth, Betsy, and Bess

Elizabeth, Elspeth, Betsy, and Bess,
They all went together to seek a bird's nest;
They found a bird's nest with five eggs in,
They all took one, and left four in.

# Little Bo-Peep

Little Bo–Peep has lost her sheep,
And can't tell where to find them;
Leave them alone, and they'll
   come home,
Wagging their tails behind them.

Little Bo–Peep fell fast asleep,
And dreamt she heard them
   bleating;
But when she awoke, she found
   it a joke,
For still they all were fleeting.

Then up she took her little crook,
Determined for to find them;
She, found them indeed, but it
   made her heart bleed,

For they'd left all their
   tails behind 'em!
It happened one day, as
   Bo–peep did stray
Unto a meadow
   hard by—
There she espied
   their tails, side
   by side,
All hung on a tree to dry.

She heaved a sigh and wiped
   her eye,
And over the hillocks she raced;
And tried what she could, as a
   shepherdess should,
That each tail should be properly
   placed.

# Over the Water

Over the water, and over the sea,
And over the water to Charley,
I'll have none of your nasty beef,
Nor I'll have none of your barley;
But I'll have some of your very best flour
To make a white cake for my Charley.

# The Farmer and the Raven

A farmer went trotting upon his gray mare,
Bumpety, bumpety, bump!
With his daughter behind him so rosy and fair,
Lumpety, lumpety, lump!

A raven cried "croak!" and they all tumbled down,
Bumpety, bumpety, bump!
The mare broke her knees, and the
farmer his crown,
Lumpety, lumpety, lump!

The mischievous raven
flew laughing away,
Bumpety, bumpety, bump!
And vowed he would serve
them the same the next day,
Lumpety, lumpety lump!

# Old Mother Goose

Old Mother Goose
When she wanted to wander,
Would ride through the air
On a very fine gander.

# Ride a Cock–Horse

Ride a cock–horse to Banbury Cross,
To see a fine lady upon a white horse.
Rings on her fingers, and bells on her toes,
She shall have music wherever she goes.

# Rub–a–Dub–Dub

Rub–a–dub–dub
Three men in a tub,
And how do you think they got there?
The butcher, the baker, the candlestick maker,
They all jumped out of a rotten potato,
'Twas enough to make a man stare.

# Sneezing

If you sneeze on Monday, you sneeze for danger;

Sneeze on a Tuesday, kiss a stranger;

Sneeze on a Wednesday, sneeze for a letter;

Sneeze on a Thursday, something better.

Sneeze on a Friday, sneeze for sorrow;

Sneeze on a Saturday, joy tomorrow.

# Georgie Porgie

Georgie Porgie, pudding and pie,
Kissed the girls and made them cry.
When the boys came out to play,
Georgie Porgie ran away.

# Handy Pandy

Handy Pandy, Jack–a–dandy,
Loves plum cake and sugar candy.
He bought some at a grocer's shop,
And out he came, hop, hop, hop!

# Little Tom Tucker

Little Tom Tucker
Sings for his supper.
What shall he eat?
White bread and butter.
How will he cut it
Without ever a knife?
How will he be married
Without ever a wife?

# I Had a Little Husband

I had a little husband no bigger than my thumb,
I put him in a pint pot, and there I bid him drum.
I bought a little handkerchief to wipe his little nose,
And a pair of little garters to tie his little hose.

# The Old Woman in the Shoe

There was an old woman who lived
    in a shoe.
She had so many children, she didn't
    know what to do.
She gave them some broth without any bread.
She whipped them all soundly and put them to bed.

# Buttons

Buttons, a farthing a pair!
Come, who will buy them of me?
They're round and sound and pretty,
And fit for girls of the city.
Come, who will buy them of me?
Buttons, a farthing a pair!

# If I Had a Donkey

If I had a donkey
That wouldn't go
Do you think I'd beat him?
Oh, no, no!
I'd put him in a barn
And give him some corn,
The best little donkey
That ever was born.

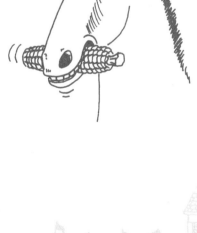

# A Tisket, a Tasket

A tisket, a tasket,
A green and yellow basket,
I wrote a letter to my love,
And on the way, I dropped it.

I dropped it, I dropped it,
And on the way I dropped it.
A little boy picked it up
And put it in his pocket.

# Little Jenny Wren

Little Jenny Wren fell sick,
Upon a time;
In came Robin Redbreast
And brought her cake and wine.

"Eat well of my cake, Jenny,
Drink well of my wine."
"Thank you, Robin, kindly,
You shall be mine."

Jenny she got well,
And stood upon her feet,
And told Robin plainly
She loved him not a bit.

Robin being angry,
Hopped upon a twig,
Saying, "Out upon you! Fie upon you!
Bold-faced jig!"

# Lock and Key

"I am a gold lock."

"I am a gold key."

"I am a silver lock."

"I am a silver key."

"I am a brass lock."

"I am a brass key."

"I am a lead lock."

"I am a lead key."

"I am a don lock."

"I am a don key!"

# Little Boy Blue

Little Boy Blue, come, blow your horn!
The sheep's in the meadow, the cow's
    in the corn.
Where's the little boy who looks
    after the sheep?
Under the haystack,
    fast asleep!

# Twelve Pairs

Twelve pairs hanging high,
Twelve knights riding by,
Each knight took a pear,
And yet left a dozen there.

# Winken, Blinken, and Nod

Winken, Blinken, and Nod one night
Sailed off in a wooden shoe,
Sailed off on a river of crystal light,
Into a sea of dew.

"Where are you going, and what
   do you wish?"
The old moon asked the three.
"We have come to fish for the herring fish
That live in the beautiful sea;
Nets of silver and gold have we!"
Said Winken,
Blinken,
And Nod.

The old moon laughed and sang a song,
As they rocked in the wooden shoe,
And the wind that sped them all night long
Ruffled the waves of dew.

The little stars were the herring fish
That lived in the beautiful sea.
"Now cast your nets wherever you wish—
Never afeard are we";
So cried the stars to the fisherman three:
Winken,
Blinken,
And Nod.

All night long their nets they threw
To the stars in the twinkling foam—
Then down from the skies came the
   wooden shoe
Bringing the fisherman home;
T'was all so pretty a sail it seemed
As if it could not be,
And some folks though t'was a dream
   they'd dreamed
Of sailing that beautiful sea—

But I shall name you the fisherman three:
Winken,
Blinken,
And Nod.

Winken and Blinken are two little eyes,
And Nod is a little head,
And the wooden shoes that sailed the skies
Is the wee one's trundle–bed.

So shut your eyes while mother sings
Of wonderful sights that be,
And you shall see the beautiful things
As you rock in the misty sea,
Where the old shoe rocked the
    fisherman three:
Winken,
Blinken,
And Nod.

# Robin and Richard

Robin and Richard were two pretty men,
They lay in bed till the clock struck ten;
Then up starts Robin and looks at the sky,
"Oh, brother Richard, the sun's very high!
You go before, with the bottle and bag,
And I will come after on little Jack nag."

# Robin Hood and Little John

Robin Hood, Robin Hood,
Is in the mickle wood!
Little John, Little John,
He to the town is gone.

Robin Hood, Robin Hood,
Telling his beads,
All in the greenwood
Among the green weeds.

Little John, Little John,
If he comes no more,
Robin Hood, Robin Hood,
We shall fret full sore!

# As I Was Going to St. Ives

As I was going to St. Ives

I met a man with seven wives.

Every wife had seven sacks,

Every sack had seven cats,

Every cat had seven kits.

Kits, cats, sacks, and wives,

How many were going to St. Ives?

# Humpty Dumpty

Humpty Dumpty sat on a wall,
Humpty Dumpty had a great fall;
All the King's horses, and all the King's men
Couldn't put Humpty together again.

# See a Pin

See a pin and pick it up,

All the day you'll have good luck.

See a pin and let it lay,

Bad luck you'll have all the day.

# Here Sits the Lord Mayor

Here sits the Lord Mayor,
Here sit his two men,
Here sits the cock,
Here sits the hen,
Here sit the little chickens,
Here they run in.
Chin-chopper, chin-chopper,
Chin chopper, chin!

# Come Out to Play

Girls and boys, come out to play,

The moon doth shine as bright as day;

Leave your supper, and leave your sleep,

And come with your playfellows into the street.

Come with a whoop, come with a call,

Come with a good will or not at all.

Up the ladder and down the wall,

A halfpenny roll will serve us all.

You find milk, and I'll find flour,

And we'll have a pudding in half an hour.

# London Bridge

London Bridge is falling down,
Falling down, falling down;
London Bridge is falling down,
My fair lady.

Build it up with silver and gold,
Silver and gold, silver and gold;
Build it up with silver and gold,
My fair lady.

Silver and gold will be stolen away,
Stolen away, stolen away;
Silver and gold will be stolen away,
My fair lady.

Build it up with iron and steel,
Iron and steel, iron and steel;
Build it up with iron and steel,
My fair lady.

Iron and steel will bend and bow;
Bend and bow, bend and bow;
Iron and steel will bend and bow,
My fair lady.

Build it up with wood and clay,
Wood and clay, wood and clay;
Build it up with wood and clay,
My fair lady.

Wood and clay will wash away,
Wash away, wash away;
Wood and clay will wash away,
My fair lady.

Build it up with stone so strong,
Stone so strong, stone so strong;
Stone so strong will last so long,
My fair lady.

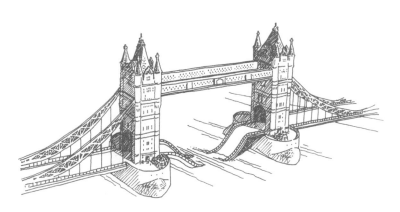

# Hector Protector

Hector Protector was dressed all in green;

Hector Protector was sent to the Queen.

The Queen did not like him,

No more did the King;

So Hector Protector was sent back again.

# Peter, Peter, Pumpkin–Eater

Peter, Peter, pumpkin–eater,
Had a wife and couldn't keep her;
He put her in a pumpkin shell,
And there he kept her
   very well.

## Elsie Marley

Elsie Marley's grown so fine,
She won't get up to feed the swine,
But lies in bed 'til eight or nine!
Lazy Elsie Marley.

# Poor Old Robinson Crusoe!

Poor old Robinson Crusoe!

Poor old Robinson Crusoe!

They made him a coat

Of an old Nanny goat.

I wonder why they should do so!

With a ring–a–ting–tang,

And a ring–a–ting–tang,

Poor old Robinson Crusoe!

# The Hobby-Horse

I had a little hobby–horse,
And it was dapple gray;
Its head was made of pea–straw,
Its tail was made of hay,
I sold it to an old woman
For a copper groat;
And I'll not sing my song again
Without another coat.

# Sing a Song of Sixpence

Sing a song of sixpence,
A pocket full of rye;
Four and twenty blackbirds
Baked in a pie.
When the pie was opened
The birds began to sing;
Was not that a dainty dish
To set before the king?

The king was in his counting house,
Counting out his money;
The queen was in the parlor,
Eating bread and honey.
The maid was in the garden,
Hanging out the clothes;
When down came a blackbird
And snipped off her nose.

# Sippity Sup

Sippity sup, sippity sup,
Bread and milk from a china cup.
Bread and milk from a bright silver spoon
Made of a piece of the bright silver moon.
Sippity sup, sippity sup,
Sippity, sippity sup.

# Hey, Diddle, Diddle

Hey, diddle, diddle!
The cat and the fiddle,
The cow jumped over
  the moon;
The little dog laughed
To see such sport,
And the dish ran away
  with the spoon.

**76**

# For Every Evil

For every evil under the sun
There is a remedy or there is none.
If there be one, seek till you find it;
If there be none, never mind it.

# The King of France

The King of France went up the hill,
With twenty thousand men;
The King of France came down the hill,
And ne'er went up again.

# Thirty Days Hath September

Thirty days hath September,

April, June, and November;

February has twenty–eight alone,

All the rest have thirty–one,

Excepting leap–year, that's the time

When February's days are twenty–nine.

# The Old Woman from France

There came an old woman from France
Who taught grown–up children to dance;
But they were so stiff,
She sent them home in a sniff,
This sprightly old woman from France.

# Wash the Dishes

Wash the dishes,
Wipe the dishes,
Ring the bell for tea;
Three good wishes,
Three good kisses,
I will give to thee.

# Rain, Rain

Rain, rain, go away,
Come again another day;
Little Johnny wants to play.

# Willy Boy

"Willy boy, Willy boy, where
   are you going?
I will go with you, if that I may."
"I'm going to the meadow to see
   them a–mowing,
I'm going to help them to make the hay."

# There Was an Old Woman Sat Spinning

There was an old woman sat spinning,
And that's the first beginning;

She had a calf,
And that's half;

She took it by the tail,
And threw it over the wall,
And that's all!

# A Plum Pudding

Flour of England, fruit of Spain,
Met together in a shower of rain;
Put in a bag tied round with a string;
If you'll tell me this riddle,
I'll give you a ring.

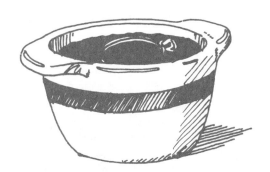

# The Piper and His Cow

There was a piper had a cow,
And he had naught to give her;
He pulled out his pipes and played her a tune,
And bade the cow consider.

The cow considered very well,
And gave the piper a penny,
And bade him play the other tune,
"Corn rigs are bonny."

# Pat–a–Cake

Pat–a–cake, pat–a–cake, baker's man!
Bake me a cake as fast as you can.
Roll it and pat it, and mark it with a B,
And put it in the oven for baby and me.

# Cobbler, Cobbler

Cobbler, cobbler, mend my shoe.
Get it done by half past two.
Half past two is much too late!
Get it done by half past eight.

# This Little Froggy

This little froggy took a big leap,
This little froggy took a small,
This little froggy leaped sideways,
And this little froggy not at all,
And this little froggy went,
Hippity, hippity, hippity hop, all the
    way home.

# Sleep, Baby, Sleep

Sleep, baby, sleep,
Our cottage vale is deep:
The little lamb is on the green,
With woolly fleece so soft and clean—
Sleep, baby, sleep.

Sleep, baby, sleep,
Down where the woodbines creep;
Be always like the lamb so mild,
A kind, and sweet, and gentle child.
Sleep, baby, sleep.

# Pease Porridge Hot

Pease porridge hot,

Pease porridge cold,

Pease porridge in the pot,

Nine days old.

Some like it hot,

Some like it cold,

Some like it in the pot,

Nine days old.

# Taffy Was a Welshman

Taffy was a Welshman, Taffy was a thief,

Taffy came to my house and stole a piece of beef.

I went to Taffy's house, Taffy was not home;

Taffy came to my house and stole a mutton bone.

I went to Taffy's house, Taffy was not in;

Taffy came to my house and stole a silver pin;

I went to Taffy's house, Taffy was in bed,

I took up the mutton bone and flung it at his head.

# Tweedle–Dum
# and Tweedle–Dee

Tweedle–dum and Tweedle–dee
Resolved to have a battle,
For Tweedle–dum
    said Tweedle–dee
Had spoiled his nice
    new rattle.

Just then flew by a
    monstrous crow,
As big as a tar barrel,
Which frightened both the heroes so,
They quite forgot their quarrel.

# There Was a Little Turtle

There was a little turtle
Who lived in a box.
He swam in the puddles
And climbed on the rocks.
He snapped at the mosquito,
He snapped at the flea.
He snapped at the minnow,
And he snapped at **me**.
He caught the mosquito,
He caught the flea.
He caught the minnow,
But he didn't catch me!

# Old King Cole

Old King Cole
Was a merry old soul,
And a merry old soul was he;

He called for his pipe,
And he called for his bowl,
And he called for his fiddlers three!

Every fiddler had a fine fiddle;
A very fine fiddle had he,
Tweedle dum, tweedle dee,
Tweedle dum, tweedle dee,
Tweedle dum went the
    fiddlers three.

# When I Was a Little Girl

When I was a little girl, about
    seven years old,
I hadn't got a petticoat, to
    cover me from the cold.

So I went into Darlington, that
    pretty little town,
And there I bought a petticoat,
    a cloak, and a gown.
I went into the woods and built
    me a kirk,
And all the birds of the air,
    they helped me to work.
The hawk with his long claws
    pulled down the stone,
The dove with her rough bill
    brought me them home.
The parrot was the clergyman,
    the peacock was the clerk,
The bullfinch played the organ,
    and we made merry work.

# The Alphabet

A, B, C, and D,

Pray, playmates, agree.

E, F, and G,

Well, so it shall be.

J, K, and L,

In peace we will dwell.

M, N, and 0,

To play let us go.

P, Q, R, and S,

Love may we possess.

W, X, and Y,

Will not quarrel or die.

Z, and ampersand,

Go to school at command.

# Diddle, Diddle, Dumpling

Diddle, diddle, dumpling, my son John
Went to bed with his trousers on,
One shoe off, and one shoe on;
Diddle, diddle, dumpling, my son John.

# Doctor Fell

I do not like thee, Doctor Fell;
The reason why I cannot tell;
But this I know, and know full well,
I do not like thee, Doctor Fell!

# Little Jack Horner

Little Jack Horner
Sat in the corner,
Eating a Christmas pie:
He put in his thumb,
And pulled out a plum,
And said, "What a good boy am I!"

# Butterfly, Butterfly

Butterfly, butterfly,
Whence do you come?
"I know not, I ask not,
Nor ever had a home."
Butterfly, butterfly,
Where do you go?
"Where the sun shines,
And where the buds grow."

98

# Lend Me Thy Mare
# to Ride a Mile

"Lend me thy mare to ride a mile."
"She is lamed, leaping over a stile."

"Alack, and I must keep the fair!
I'll give the money for thy mare."

"Oh, oh! Say you so?
Money will make the mare to go!"

# The Old Woman of Gloucester

There was an old woman
of Gloucester,
Whose parrot two guineas it
cost her,
But its tongue never ceasing,
Was vastly displeasing
To the talkative woman
of Gloucester.

# Pussycat Sits by the Fire

Pussycat sits by the fire;
How can she be fair?
In walks the little dog;
Says: "Pussy, are you there?
How do you do, Mistress Pussy?
Mistress Pussy, how do you do?"
"I thank you kindly, little dog,
I fare as well as you!"

# The House that Jack Built

This is the house that Jack built.
This is the malt
That lay in the house that Jack built.

This is the rat,
That ate the malt
That lay in the house that Jack built.

This is the cat,
That killed the rat,
That ate the malt
That lay in the house that Jack built.

This is the dog,
That worried the cat,
That killed the rat,
That ate the malt
That lay in the house
   that Jack built.

This is the cow with the crumpled horn,
That tossed the dog,
That worried the cat,
That killed the rat,
That ate the malt
That lay in the house that Jack built.

This is the maiden all forlorn,
That milked the cow with the crumpled horn,
That tossed the dog,
That worried the cat,
That killed the rat,
That ate the malt
That lay in the house that Jack built.

This is the man all tattered and torn,
That kissed the maiden all forlorn,
That milked the cow with the crumpled horn,
      That tossed the dog,

That worried the cat,

That killed the rat,

That ate the malt

That lay in the house that Jack built.

This is the priest all shaven and shorn,

That married the man all tattered and torn,

That kissed the maiden all forlorn,

That milked the cow with the crumpled horn,

That tossed the dog,

That worried the cat,

That killed the rat,

That ate the malt

That lay in the house that Jack built.

This is the cock that crowed in the morn,

That waked the priest all shaven and shorn,

That married the man all tattered and torn,

That kissed the maiden all forlorn,

That milked the cow with the crumpled horn,

That tossed the dog,

That worried the cat,

That killed the rat,

That ate the malt

That lay in the house that Jack built.

This is the farmer sowing the corn,

That kept the cock that crowed in the morn,

That waked the priest all shaven and shorn,

That married the man all tattered and torn,

That kissed the maiden all forlorn,

That milked the cow with the crumpled horn,

That tossed the dog,

That worried the cat,

That killed the rat,

That ate the malt

That lay in the house that Jack built.

# Dickory, Dickory, Dare

Dickory, dickory, dare,
The pig flew up in the air;
The man in brown
Soon brought him down,
Dickory, dickory, dare.

# Fiddle Dee Dee

Fiddle dee dee, fiddle dee dee,

The fly has married the bumblebee.

They went to the church,

And married was she.

The fly has married the bumblebee.

# Doctor Foster

Doctor Foster went to Gloucester,
In a shower of rain;
He stepped in a puddle
Right up to his middle,
And never went there again.

# Goosey, Goosey, Gander

Goosey, goosey, gander,
Where shall I wander?
Upstairs and downstairs
And in my lady's chamber.

There I met an old man
Who wouldn't say his prayers;
I took him by the left leg,
And threw him down the stairs.

# If All the Seas
# Were One Sea

If all the seas were one sea,
What a great sea that would be!
And if all the trees were one tree,
What a great tree that would be!
And if all the axes were one axe,
What a great axe that would be!
And if all the men were one man,
What a great man he would be!
And if the great man took the great axe,
And cut down the great tree,
And let it fall into the great sea,
What a splish splash that would be!

# Ding, Dong, Bell

Ding, dong, bell,
Pussy's in the well!
Who put her in?
Little Johnny Green.
Who pulled her out?
Little Tommy Stout.
What a naughty boy was that,
To try to drown poor pussycat.
Who never did him any harm,
And killed the mice in his father's barn!

# I Had a Little Nut Tree

I had a little nut tree,
Nothing would it bear,
But a silver nutmeg and a golden pear.
The King of Spain's daughter
Came to see me,
All because of my little nut tree.
I skipped over water,
I danced over sea,
And all the birds in the air couldn't
catch me.

# One, Two, Buckle My Shoe

One, two,
Buckle my shoe;
Three, four,
Knock at the door;
Five, six,
Pick up sticks;
Seven, eight,
Lay them straight;
Nine, ten,
A good, fat hen;

Eleven, twelve,
Dig and delve;
Thirteen, fourteen,
Maids a–courting;
Fifteen, sixteen,
Maids in the kitchen;
Seventeen, eighteen,
Maids a–waiting;
Nineteen, twenty,
I've had plenty.

# There Was a Little Boy
# and a Little Girl

There was a little boy and a little girl
Lived in an alley;
Says the little boy to the little girl,
"Shall I, oh, shall I?"

Says the little girl to the little boy,
"What shall we do?"
Says the little boy to the little girl,
"I will kiss you."

# Hot Cross Buns

Hot cross buns!
Hot cross buns!
One a penny, two a penny,
Hot cross buns!

If you have no daughters,
Give them to your sons.
One a penny, two a penny,
Hot cross buns!

# Who Killed Cock Robin?

Who killed Cock Robin?
"I," said the sparrow,
"With my little bow and arrow,
I killed Cock Robin."

Who saw him die?
"I," said the fly,
"With my little eye,
I saw him die."

Who caught his blood?
"I," said the fish,
"With my little dish,
I caught his blood."

Who'll make his shroud?
"I," said the beetle,
"With my thread and needle.
I'll make his shroud."

Who'll carry the torch?
"I," said the linnet,
"I'll come in a minute,
I'll carry the torch."

Who'll be the clerk?
"I," said the lark,
"If it's not in the dark,
I'll be the clerk."

Who'll dig his grave?
"I," said the owl,
"With my spade and trowel
I'll dig his grave."

Who'll be the parson?
"I," said the rook,
"With my little book,
I'll be the parson."

Who'll be chief mourner?
"I," said the dove,
"I mourn for my love,
I'll be chief mourner."

Who'll sing a psalm?
"I," said the thrush,

"As I sit in a bush.
I'll sing a psalm."

Who'll carry the coffin?
"I," said the kite,
"If it's not in the night,
I'll carry the coffin."

Who'll toll the bell?
"I," said the bull,
"Because I can pull,
I'll toll the bell."
All the birds of the air
Fell sighing and sobbing,
When they heard the bell toll
For poor Cock Robin.

# Tom, Tom, the Piper's Son

Tom, Tom, the piper's son,
Stole a pig, and away he run,
The pig was eat,
And Tom was beat,
And Tom ran crying down the street.

# Hick–a–More, Hack–a–More

Hick–a–more, Hack–a–more,
On the King's kitchen door,
All the King's horses,
And all the King's men,
Couldn't drive Hick–a–more,
    Hack–a–more,
Off the King's kitchen door.

# The Derby Ram

As I was going to Derby all on a market–day,

I met the finest ram, sir, that ever was fed upon hay;

Upon hay, upon hay, upon hay;

I met the finest ram, sir, that ever was fed upon hay.

This ram was fat behind, sir; this ram was fat before;

This ram was ten yards round, sir; indeed, he was
   no more;

No more, no more, no more;

This ram was ten yards round, sir; indeed, he was
no more.

The horns that grew on his head, they were so
wondrous high,

As I've been plainly told, sir; they reached up to
the sky.

The sky, the sky, the sky;

As I've been plainly told, sir, they reached up to
the sky.

The tail that grew from his back, sir, was six yards
and an ell;

And it was sent to Derby to toll the market bell;

The bell, the bell, the bell;

And it was sent to Derby to toll the market bell.

# Pussycat, Pussycat

"Pussycat, pussycat,
Where have you been?"
"I've been to London
To look at the Queen."

"Pussycat, pussycat,
What did you there?"
I frightened a little mouse
Under the chair."

# Myself

As I walked by myself,
And talked to myself,
Myself said unto me:
"Look to thyself,
Take care of thyself,
For nobody cares for thee."

I answered myself,
And said to myself
In the selfsame repartee:
"Look to thyself,
Or not look to thyself,
The selfsame thing will be."

# Monday's Child

Monday's child is fair of face,

Tuesday's child is full of grace,

Wednesday's child is full of woe,

Thursday's child has far to go.

Friday's child is loving and giving,

Saturday's child works hard for his living;

But the child that's born on the Sabbath day,

Is fair and wise and good and gay.

# Where Are You Going, My Pretty Maid

"Where are you going, my pretty maid?"
"I'm going a–milking, sir," she said.
"May I go with you, my pretty maid?"
"You're kindly welcome, sir," she said.
"What is your father, my pretty maid?"
"My father's a farmer, sir," she said.
"What is your fortune, my pretty maid?"
"My face is my fortune, sir," she said.
"Then I can't marry you, my pretty maid."
"Nobody asked you, sir," she said.

# In Marble Walls

In marble walls as white as milk,
Lined with skin as soft as silk;
Within a fountain crystal clear,
A golden apple doth appear.
No doors there are to this stronghold—
Yet thieves break in and steal the gold.

# Little Jumping Joan

Here am I, little jumping Joan,
When nobody's with me
I'm always alone.

# Jack Be Nimble

Jack be nimble,
Jack be quick,
Jack jump over
the candlestick.

# The Little Moppet

I had a little moppet,
I put it in my pocket,
And fed it with corn and hay.
There came a proud beggar,
And swore he should have her;
And stole my little moppet away.

# For Want of a Nail

For want of a nail, the shoe was lost;
For want of the shoe, the horse was lost;
For want of the horse, the rider was lost;
For want of the rider, the battle was lost;
For want of the battle, the kingdom was lost,
And all for the want of a horseshoe nail.

# The Mulberry Bush

Here we go round the mulberry bush,
The mulberry bush, the mulberry bush,
Here we go round the mulberry bush,
On a cold and frosty morning.

This is the way we wash our hands,
Wash our hands, wash our hands,
This is the way we wash our hands,
On a cold and frosty morning.

This is the way we wash our clothes,
Wash our clothes, wash our clothes,
This is the way we wash our clothes,
On a cold and frosty morning.

This is the way we go to school,
Go to school, go to school,
This is the way we go to school,
On a cold and frosty morning.

This is the way we come out of school,
Come out of school, come out of school,
This is the way we come out of school,
On a cold and frosty morning.

# Master I Have

Master I have, and I am his man,
Gallop a dreary dun;
Master I have, and I am his man,
And I'll get a wife as fast as I can;
With a heighty gaily gamberally,
Higgledy piggledy,
   niggledy, niggledy,
Gallop a dreary dun.

# The Little Mouse

I have seen you, little mouse,
Running all about the house,
Through the hole your little eye
In the wainscot peeping sly,
Hoping soon some crumbs to steal,
To make quite a hearty meal.
Look before you venture out,
See if pussy is about.
If she's gone, you'll quickly run
To the larder for some fun;
Round about the dishes creep,
Taking into each a peep,
To choose the daintiest
   that's there,
Spoiling things you do
   not care.

# Whether the Weather

Whether the weather be fine,
Or whether the weather be not,
Whether the weather be cold,
Or whether the weather be hot,
We'll weather the weather
Whatever the weather,
Whether we like it or not!

# Jack Sprat

Jack Sprat
Could eat no fat,
His wife could eat no lean;
And so, between them both, you see,
They licked the platter clean.

# Wee Willie Winkie

Wee Willie Winkie runs through the town,
Upstairs and downstairs, in his nightgown;
Rapping at the window, crying through the lock,
"Are the children in their beds?
It's now eight o'clock."

# The Man of Bombay

There was a fat man of Bombay,

Who was smoking one sunshiny day,

When a bird called a snipe

Flew away with his pipe,

Which vexed the fat man of Bombay.

# As I Went To Bonner

As I went to Bonner,
I met a pig
Without a wig
Upon my word and honor.

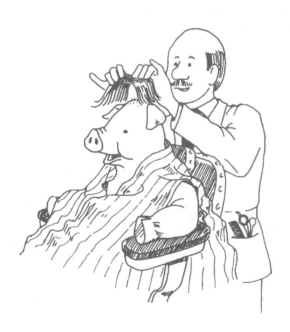

## Barber, Barber

Barber, barber, shave a pig.
How many hairs will make a wig?
Four and twenty; that's enough.
Give the barber a pinch of snuff.

# Pippen Hill

As I was going up Pippen Hill
Pippen Hill was dirty;
There I met a pretty Miss,
And she dropped me a curtsy.

Little Miss, pretty Miss,
Blessings light upon you;
If I had half–a–crown a day,
I'd spend it all upon you.

# The Old Woman of Surrey

There was an old woman of Surrey,
Who was morn, noon, and night in a hurry;
Called her husband a fool,
Drove the children to school,
The worrying old woman
of Surrey.

# Hickety, Pickety

Hickety, pickety, my black hen,
She lays eggs for gentlemen;
Gentlemen come every day
To see what my black hen doth lay.
Sometimes nine and sometimes ten,
Hickety, pickety, my
   black hen.

# Willy, Willy

Willy, Willy Wilkin
Kissed the maids a–milking,
Fa, la, la!
And with his merry daffing
    He set them all a–laughing,
       Ha, ha, ha!

# Horsie, Horsie, Don't You Stop

Horsie, horsie, don't you stop,
    Just let your feet go clippety clop;

    Your tail goes swish,
        And the wheels go round—
        Giddyup, you're
           homeward bound!

# The Blacksmith

"Robert Barnes, my fellow fine,

Can you shoe this horse of mine?"

"Yes, good sir, that I can,

As well as any other man;

    There's a nail, and there's a prod,

        Now, good sir, your horse

          is shod."

# One Misty Moisty Morning

One misty moisty morning,
When cloudy was
    the weather,
I chanced to meet
    an old man,
Clothed all in leather.
He began to compliment
And I began to grin.
"How do you do?"
And "How do you do?"
And "How do you do again?"

# Three Young Rats

Three young rats with black felt hats,

Three young ducks with white straw flats,

Three young dogs with curling tails,

Three young cats with demi–veils,

Went out to walk with two young pigs

In satin vests and sorrel wigs.

But suddenly it began to rain

And so they all went home again.

# One For Sorrow

One for sorrow,

Two for joy,

Three for a girl,

Four for a boy,

Five for silver,

Six for gold,

Seven for a secret

Never to be told.

# The Man Who Had Naught

There was a man and he had naught,

And robbers came to rob him;

He crept up to the chimney pot,

And then they thought they had him.

But he got down on the other side,

And then they could not find him;

He ran fourteen miles in fifteen days,

And never looked behind him.

# I Love Sixpence

I love sixpence, a jolly, jolly sixpence,

I love sixpence as my life;

I spent a penny of it, I spent a

    penny of it,

I took a penny home to

    my Wife.


Oh, my little

    fourpence, a jolly,

    jolly fourpence,

I love fourpence as my life;

I spent twopence of it, I spent

    twopence of it,

And I took twopence home to my wife.

# The Clock

There's a neat little clock,—
In the schoolroom it stands,—
And it points to the time
With its two little hands.

And may we, like the clock,
Keep a face clean and bright,
With hands ever ready
To do what is right.

# Just Like Me

"I went up one pair of stairs."
"Just like me."

"I went up two pairs of stairs."
"Just like me."

"I went into a room."
"Just like me."

"I looked out of
    a window."
"Just like me."

"And there I saw
    a monkey."
"Just like me."

# The Man in the Moon

The Man in the Moon came tumbling down,
And asked the way to Norwich;
He went by the south, and burnt his mouth
By eating hot pease porridge.

# A Wise Old Owl

A wise old owl sat in an oak,
The more he heard, the less
    he spoke;
The less he spoke, the
    more he heard;
Why aren't we all like that wise old bird.

# Dance, Thumbkin, Dance

Dance, Thumbkin, dance;
Dance, ye merrymen, everyone.
For Thumbkin, he
can dance alone,
Thumbkin, he can
 dance alone.
Dance, Foreman, dance;
Dance, ye merrymen, everyone.
　　But Foreman, he can
　　　　dance alone,
　　　　　Foreman, he can
　　　　　　dance alone.
　　　　　　 Dance,
　　　　　　Longman, dance;

Dance, ye merrymen, everyone.
For Longman, he can dance alone,
Longman, he can dance alone.
Dance, Ringman, dance;
Dance, ye merrymen, dance.
But Ringman cannot dance alone,
Ringman, he cannot dance alone.
Dance, Littleman, dance;
Dance, ye merrymen, dance.
　　　　But Littleman, he can
　　　　　dance alone,
　　　　　　Littleman he can
　　　　　　dance alone.

# Two Pigeons

I had two pigeons bright and gay,
They flew from me the other day.
What was the reason they did go?
I cannot tell, for I do not know.

# Birds of a Feather

Birds of a feather flock together,
And so will pigs and swine;
Rats and mice will have their choice,
And so will I have mine.

# Saturday Night, Sunday Morning

On Saturday night
Shall be all my care
To powder my locks
And curl my hair.

On Sunday morning
My love will come in,
When he will marry me
With a gold ring.

# When Jenny Wren Was Young

'Twas once upon a time, when Jenny Wren was young,

So daintily she danced and so prettily she sung,

Robin Redbreast lost his heart, for he was a gallant bird.

So he doffed his hat to Jenny Wren, requesting to be heard.


"Oh, dearest Jenny Wren, if you will but be mine,

You shall feed on cherry pie and drink new currant wine,

I'll dress you like a goldfinch or any peacock gay,

So, dearest Jen, if you'll be mine, let us appoint the day."

Jenny blushed behind her fan and thus declared her mind:

"Since, dearest Bob, I love you well, I'll take your offer kind.

Cherry pie is very nice and so is currant wine,

But I must wear my plain brown gown and never go too fine."

# The Lost Shoe

Doodle doodle doo,
The Princess lost her shoe:
Her Highness hopped,—
The fiddler stopped,
Not knowing what to do.

# One, He Loves

One, he loves; two, he loves:
Three, he loves, they say;
Four, he loves with all
    his heart,
Five, he casts away.
Six, he loves; seven,
    she loves;
Eight, they both love.
Nine, he comes; ten,
    he tarries;
Eleven, he courts;
    twelve,
    he marries.

# Shoe the Colt

Shoe the colt,

Shoe the colt,

Shoe the wild mare;

Here a nail,

There a nail,

Yet she goes bare.

# Dame Trot and Her Cat

Dame Trot and her cat
Led a peaceable life,
When they were not troubled
With other folks' strife.

When Dame had her dinner
Pussy would wait,
And was sure to receive
A nice piece from her plate.

# When

When I was a bachelor
    I lived by myself;
        And all the bread and cheese I got
        I laid up on the shelf.

            The rats and the mice
                They made such a strife,
                    I was forced to go
                        to London
                    To buy me a wife.

                The streets were
                    so bad,
                        And the lanes were
                        so narrow,
                        I was forced to bring my
                        wife home
                    In a wheelbarrow.

    The wheelbarrow broke,
        And my wife had a fall;
            Down came wheelbarrow,
                Little wife and all.

# The Old Woman
# Under a Hill

There was an old woman
Lived under a hill;
And if she's not gone,
She lives there still.

# Pussycat Mew

Pussycat Mew jumped over a coal,
And in her best petticoat burnt a great hole.
Poor Pussy's weeping, she'll have no more milk
Until her best petticoat's mended with silk.

# Up the Wooden Hill
## to Blanket Fair

Up the wooden hill to Blanket Fair,

What shall we have when we get there?

A bucket full of water,

And a pennyworth of hay,

Gee up, Dobbin, all

   the way!

# Young Roger and Dolly

Young Roger came tapping at Dolly's window,
Thumpety, thumpety, thump!

He asked for admittance; she answered
 him "No!"
Frumpety, frumpety,
    frump!

"No, no, Roger, no!
    as you came you
    may go!"
Stumpety, stumpety,
    stump!

# Twenty Nails

Every lady in this land
Has twenty nails, upon each hand
Five, and twenty on hands and feet:
All this is true, without deceit.

# The Lion and the Unicorn

The lion and the unicorn were fighting for the crown,
The lion beat the unicorn all around the town.
Some gave them white bread, and some gave them brown,
Some gave them plum cake, and sent them out of town.

# If Wishes Were Horses

If wishes were horses, beggars would ride.

If turnips were watches, I would wear one by my side.

And if "ifs" and "ands"

Were pots and pans,

There'd be no work for tinker's hands.

# As I Was Going Along

As I was going along, along,
A–singing a comical song, song, song,
The lane that I went was so long, long, long,
  And the song that I sang was so
  long, long, long,
   And so I went singing along.

# The Old Woman of Harrow

There was an old woman of Harrow,

Who visited in a wheelbarrow;

And her servant before,

Knocked loud at each door,

To announce the old

woman of Harrow.

# The Robin

The north wind doth blow,
And we shall have snow,
And what will poor robin do then,
Poor thing?

He'll sit in a barn,
And keep himself warm,
And hide his head
under his wing,
Poor thing!

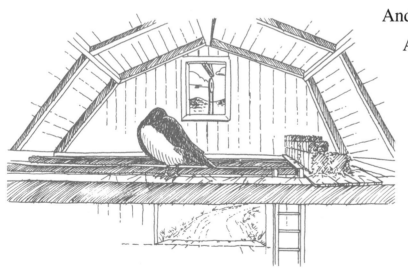

# Young Lambs to Sell

If I'd as much money as I could tell,

I never would cry young lambs to sell;

Young lambs to sell, young lambs to sell;

I never would cry young

lambs to sell.

# Ladybird

Ladybird, ladybird, fly away home!

Your house is on fire, your children all gone,

All but one, and her name is Ann,

And she crept under the pudding pan.

# Cock-a-Doodle-Do!

Cock–a–doodle–do!
My dame has lost her shoe,
 My master's lost his fiddle–stick
 And knows not what to do.

 Cock–a–doodle–do!
 What is my dame to do?
 Till master finds his fiddle–stick,
She'll dance without her shoe.

# As I Was Going to Sell My Eggs

As I was going to sell my eggs
I met a man with bandy legs,
Bandy legs and crooked toes;
I tripped up his heels, and he fell
on his nose.

# There Was a Maid on Scrabble Hill

There was a maid on Scrabble Hill,
And, if not dead, she lives there still.
She grew so tall, she reached the sky,
And on the moon hung clothes to dry.

# To Babylon

How many miles to Babylon?—
Threescore miles and ten.
Can I get there by candle–light?
Yes, and back again.
If your heels are nimble and light,
You may get there by candle–light.

# The Man of Tobago

There was an old man of Tobago

Who lived on rice, gruel, and sago,

Till much to his bliss,

His physician said this:

"To a leg, sir, of mutton, you may go."

# My Little Old Man
# and I Fell Out

My little old man and I fell out;

I'll tell you what 'twas all about,

I had money and he had none,

And that's the way the noise begun.

# Smiling Girls, Rosy Boys

Smiling girls, rosy boys,

Come and buy my little toys;

Monkeys made of gingerbread,

And sugar horses painted red.

# One, Two, Three

One, two, three, four, five,

Once I caught a fish alive.

Six, seven, eight, nine, ten,

But I let it go again.

Why did you let it go?

Because it bit my finger so.

Which finger did it bite?

The little one upon
   the right.

# Bessy Bell and Mary Gray

Bessy Bell and Mary Gray,
They were two bonny lasses;
They built their house upon the lea,
And covered it with rushes.

Bessy kept the garden gate,
And Mary kept the pantry;
Bessy always had to wait,
While Mary lived in plenty.

# The Cock's on the Housetop

The cock's on the housetop blowing his horn;
The bull's in the barn a–threshing of corn;
The maids in the meadows are making of hay;
The ducks in the river are swimming away.

# Oh, My Pretty Cock

Oh, my pretty cock, oh, my handsome cock,
I pray you, do not crow before day,
And your comb shall be made of the very
    beaten gold,
And your wings of the silver so gray.

# Robin–a–Bobbin

Robin–a–Bobbin
Bent his bow,
Shot at a pigeon,
And killed a crow.

# Mother, May I Go
# Out to Swim?

"Mother, may I go out to swim?"
"Yes, my darling daughter.
Fold your clothes up neat and trim,
But don't go near the water."

# Bobby Shaftoe

Bobby Shaftoe's gone to sea,
Silver buckles on his knee:
He'll come back and marry me,
Pretty Bobby Shaftoe!

Bobby Shaftoe's fine and fair,
Combing down his yellow hair;
He's my love for evermore,
Pretty Bobby Shaftoe.

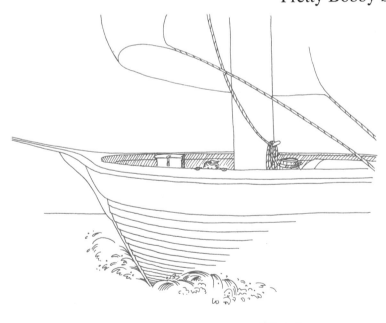

# Mary Had a Pretty Bird

Mary had a pretty bird,
With feathers bright and yellow,
Slender legs—upon my word
He was a pretty fellow!

The sweetest note he always sung,
Which much delighted Mary.
She often, where the cage was hung,
Sat hearing her canary.

# Cut Thistles in May

Cut thistles in May,
They'll grow in a day;
Cut them in June,
That is too soon;
Cut them in July,
Then they will die.

# The Old Man

There was an old man
In a velvet coat,
He kissed a maid
And gave her a groat.
The groat it was crack'd
And would not go,—
Ah, old man, do you serve me so?

# My Little Maid

High diddle doubt, my candle's out
My little maid is not at home;
Saddle my hog and bridle my dog,
And fetch my little maid home.

# I Sing, I Sing

I sing, I sing,
From morn till night;
From cares I'm free,
And my heart is light.

# Pancake Day

Great A, little a,

This is pancake day;

Toss the ball high,

Throw the ball low,

Those that come after

May sing heigh–ho!

# Dance, Little Baby

Dance, little baby, dance up high!
Never mind, baby, mother is by.
Crow and caper, caper and crow,
There, little baby, there you go!
Up to the ceiling, down
    to the ground,
Backwards and
forwards, round
and round;
Dance, little baby and
    mother will sing,
With the merry coral, ding,
    ding, ding!

# Swan

Swan swam over the sea,
Swim, swan, swim!
Swan, swan, back again,
Well swum, swan!

# The First of May

The fair maid who, the first of May,
Goes to the fields at break of day,
And washes in dew from the hawthorn–tree,
Will ever after handsome be.

# What Did I Dream?

What did I dream?
I do not know;
The fragments fly like chaff.
Yet strange my mind
Was tickled so,
I cannot help but laugh.

# Punch and Judy

Punch and Judy
Fought for a pie;
Punch gave Judy
A knock in the eye.
Says Punch to Judy,
"Will you have any more?"
Says Judy to Punch,
"My eye is too sore."

# Two Birds

There were two birds sat on a stone,

Fa, la, la, la, lal, de;

One flew away, and then there was one,

Fa, la, la, la, lal, de;

The other bird flew after,

And then there was none,

Fa, la, la, la, lal, de;

And so the stone

Was left alone,

Fa la, la, la, lal, de.

# In a Cottage in Fife

In a cottage in Fife
Lived a man and his wife
Who, believe me, were comical folk;
For, to people's surprise,
They both saw with their eyes,
And their tongues moved whenever they spoke!

When they were asleep,
I'm told, that to keep
Their eyes open they could
   not contrive;
They both walked on their feet,
And 'twas thought what they eat
Helped, with drinking, to keep,
   them alive!

# Jack Jingle

Little Jack Jingle,

He used to live single;

But when he got tired of this kind of life,

He left off being single and lived with his wife.

Now what do you think of little Jack Jingle?

Before he was married he used to live single.

# Sing, Sing

Sing, Sing, what shall I sing?
Cat's run away with the pudding–string!
Do, do, what shall I do?
The cat's run away with the pudding, too!

# The Boy in the Barn

A little boy went, into a barn,
And lay down on some hay.
An owl came out, and flew about,
And the little boy ran away.

# A Little Cock-Sparrow

A little cock–sparrow sat on a green tree,
And he chirruped, he chirruped, so merry was he;
A naughty boy came with his wee bow and arrow,
Determined to shoot this little cock–sparrow.
"This little cock–sparrow shall make me a stew,
And his giblets shall make me a little pie, too."
"Oh, no," says the sparrow
   "I won't make a stew."
So he flapped his wings and
   away he flew.

# Ride Away, Ride Away

Ride away, ride away,
Johnny shall ride,
And he shall have pussycat
Tied to one side;
And he shall have little dog
Tied to the other,
And Johnny shall ride
To see his grandmother.

# Jack and His Fiddle

"Jacky, come and give me thy fiddle,
If ever thou mean to thrive."
"Nay, I'll not give my fiddle
To any man alive.

"If I should give my fiddle,
They'll think that I've gone mad;
For many a joyous day
My fiddle and I have had."

# The Hunter of Reigate

A man went a–hunting at Reigate,
And wished to leap over a high gate.
Says the owner, "Go round,
With your gun and your hound,
For you never shall leap over my gate."

# Little Fred

When little Fred went to bed,
He always said his prayers;
He kissed mama
and his papa,
And straightway
went upstairs.

# Pussycat Ate the Dumplings

Pussycat ate the dumplings, the dumplings,
Pussycat ate the dumplings.
Mamma stood by, and cried, "Oh, fie!
Why did you eat the dumplings?"

# In Spring I Look Gay

In Spring I look gay,

Decked in comely array,

In Summer more clothing I wear;

When colder it grows,

I fling off my clothes,

And in Winter quite

naked appear.

# Hot Gray Pease

Piping hot, smoking hot.
What I've got
You have not.
Hot gray pease, hot, hot, hot;
Hot gray pease, hot.

# The Man in the Wilderness

The man in the wilderness asked me,
  "How many strawberries grew in
    the sea."
  I answered him as I
  thought good,
  "As many as red herrings grew
  in the wood."

# Little Tommy Tittlemouse

Little Tommy Tittlemouse
Lived in a little house.
  He caught fishes
  In other men's ditches.

# The Old Woman of Leeds

There was an old woman of Leeds,
Who spent all her time in good deeds;
She worked for the poor
Till her fingers were sore,
This pious old woman of Leeds!

# Little Pussy

I like little Pussy,
Her coat is so warm,
And if I don't hurt her
She'll do me no harm;
So I'll not pull her tail,
Nor drive her away,
But Pussy and I
Very gently will play.

# Whistle

"Whistle, daughter, whistle;
Whistle, daughter dear."
"I cannot whistle, mammy,
I cannot whistle clear."
"Whistle, daughter, whistle;
Whistle for a pound."
"I cannot whistle, mammy,
I cannot make a sound."

# Jerry Hall

Jerry Hall,
He was so small,
A rat could eat him,
Hat and all.

# There Was an Old Woman

There was an old woman, and what do you think?
She lived upon nothing but victuals and drink;
Victuals and drink were the chief of her diet,
And yet this old woman could never be quiet.

# When the Snow Is on the Ground

The little robin grieves
When the snow is on the ground,
For the trees have no leaves,
And no berries can be found.

The air is cold, the worms are hid;
For robin here what can be done?
Let's throw around some crumbs of bread,
And then he'll live till snow is gone.

# The Greedy Man

The greedy man is he who sits
And bites bits out of plates,
Or else takes up an almanac
And gobbles all the dates.

# Little Betty Blue

Little Betty Blue lost her holiday shoe;
What shall little Betty do?
Give her another to match the other,
And then she'll walk upon two.

# The Girl in the Lane

The girl in the lane, that couldn't speak plain,
Cried, "Gobble,
    gobble, gobble":
The man on the hill that
    couldn't stand still,
Went hobble, hobble,
    hobble.

# Cross Patch

Cross patch, draw the latch,
Sit by the fire and spin;
Take a cup and drink it up,
Then call your neighbors in.

# T'Other Little Tune

I won't be my father's Jack,
I won't be my father's Jill;
I will be the fiddler's wife,
And have music when I will.
T'other little tune,
T'other little tune,
Prithee, Love, play me
T'other little tune.

# The Woman of Exeter

There dwelt an old woman at Exeter;

When visitors came it sore vexed her,

So for fear they should eat,

She locked up all her meat,

This stingy old woman of Exeter.

# Why May Not
# I Love Johnny?

Johnny shall have a new bonnet,
And Johnny shall go to the fair,
And Johnny shall have a blue ribbon
To tie up his bonny brown hair.

And why may not I love Johnny?
And why may not Johnny love me?
And why may not I love Johnny
As well as another body?

And here's a leg for a stocking,
And here's a foot for a shoe,
And he has a kiss for his daddy,
And two for his mammy, I trow.

And why may not I love Johnny?
And why may not Johnny love me?
And why may not I love Johnny
As well as another body?

# Hi! Hi! Says Anthony

Hi! Hi! says Anthony,
Puss is in the pantry,
Gnawing, gnawing,
A mutton muttonbone.
See how she tumbles it,
See how she mumbles it,
See how she tosses
The mutton muttonbone.

# Little Polly Flinders

Little Polly Flinders
  Sat among the cinders
    Warming her pretty
    little toes.
    Her mother came and
    caught her,
    And whipped her
    little daughter
  For spoiling her nice
new clothes.

# The Winds

Mister East gave a feast;
Mister North laid the cloth;
Mister West did his best;
Mister South burnt his mouth
Eating cold potato.

# Bat, Bat, Come Under My Hat

Bat, bat, come under my hat,
And I'll give you a slice of bacon;
And when I bake, I'll give you a cake
If I am not mistaken.

# About the Bush

About the bush, Willie,
About the beehive,
About the bush, Willie,
I'll meet thee alive.

# Six Little Mice

Six little mice sat down to spin;

Pussy passed by and she peeped in;

"What are you doing, my little men?"

"Weaving coats for gentlemen."

"Shall I come in and cut off your threads?"

"No, no, Mistress Pussy, you'd bite off our heads."

"Oh, no, I'll not; I'll help you to spin."

"That may be so, but you can't come in!"

# Little Poll Parrot

Little Poll Parrot
Sat in his garret
Eating toast and tea;
A little brown mouse
Jumped into the house,
And stole it all away.

# The Robins

A robin and a robin's son
Once went to town to buy a bun.
They couldn't decide on plum
   or plain,
And so they went back home again.

# A Sure Test

If you are to be a gentleman,
As I suppose you'll be,
You'll neither laugh nor smile,
For a tickling of the knee.

# My Kitten, My Kitten

Hey, my kitten, my kitten,
And hey, my kitten, my deary!
Such a sweet pet as this
Was neither far nor neary.

# Little Girl and Queen

"Little girl, little girl, where have you been?"
"Gathering roses to give to the Queen."
"Little girl, little girl, what gave she you?"
"She gave me a diamond as big as my shoe."

# Trip Upon Trenchers

Trip upon trenchers,
And dance upon dishes,
My mother sent me for some barm, some barm.

She bid me go lightly,
And come again quickly,
For fear the young men should do me
    some harm.

Yet didn't you see,
Yet didn't you see,
What naughty tricks they put
    upon me?

They broke my pitcher,
And spilt the water,
And chid her daughter,
And kissed my sister instead of me!

# The Bells of St. Helen's

"You owe me five shillings,"
Say the bells of St. Helen's.
"When will you pay me?"
Say the bells of Old Bailey.
"When I grow rich,"
Say the bells of Shoreditch.
"When will that be?"
Say the bells of Stepney.
"I do not know,"
Says the great Bell of Bow.
"Two sticks in an apple,"
Ring the bells of
    Whitechapel.
"Halfpence and farthings,"
Say the bells of St. Martin's.
"Kettles and pans,"

Say the bells of St. Ann's.
"Brickbats and tiles,"
Say the bells of St. Giles.
"Old shoes and slippers,"
Say the bells of St. Peter's.
"Pokers and tongs,"
Say the bells of St. John's.

# Away, Birds, Away

Away, birds, away!
Take a little and leave a little,
And do not come again;
For if you do,
I will shoot you through,
And there will be an end of you.

# Hush–a–Bye Baby

Hush–a–bye, baby, lie still with thy daddy,

Thy mammy has gone to the mill,

To get some meal to bake a cake,

So pray, my dear baby, lie still.

# The Man of Derby

A little old man of Derby,

How do you think he served me?

He took away my bread and cheese,

And that is how he served me.

# Billy, Billy

"Billy, Billy, come and play,
While the sun shines bright as day."

"Yes, my Polly, so I will,
For I love to please you still."

"Billy, Billy, have you seen
Sam and Betsy on the green?"

"Yes, my Poll, I saw them pass,
Skipping o'er the new–
    mown grass."

"Billy, Billy, come along,
    And I will sing a pretty song."

# The Coachman

Up at Piccadilly, oh!
The coachman takes his stand,
And when he meets a pretty girl
He takes her by the hand.
Whip away forever, oh!
Drive away so clever, oh!
All the way to Bristol, oh!
He drives her four–in–hand.

# Here Goes My Lord

Here goes my lord
A trot, a trot, a trot, a trot,
Here goes my lady
A canter, a canter, a canter, a canter!

Here goes my young master
Jockey–hitch, jockey–hitch, jockey–hitch, jockey–hitch!
Here goes my young miss
An amble, an amble, an amble,
an amble!

The footman lags behind to
tipple ale and wine,
And goes gallop, a gallop,
a gallop, to make up his time.

# Dance to Your Daddy

Dance to your daddy
My little laddie;
Dance to your daddy, my little lamb;
You shall get a fishy,
On a little dishy;
You shall get a fishy,
When the boat
   comes in.

# Little Maid

"Little maid, pretty maid, whither goest thou?"
"Down in the forest to milk my cow."
"Shall I go with thee?" "No, not now;
When I send for thee, then come thou."

# The Hart

The hart he loves the high wood,
The hare she loves the hill;
The Knight he loves his bright sword,
The Lady—loves her will.

# A Counting–Out Rhyme

Hickory, dickory, 6 and 7,
Alabone, Crackabone, 10 and 11,
Spin, spun, muskidun,
Twiddle 'em, twaddle 'em, 21.

# The Dove and the Wren

The dove says, "coo, coo, what shall I do?
I can scarce maintain two."
"Pooh, pooh!" says the wren, "I've got ten,
And keep them all like gentlemen."

# Intery, Mintery, Cutery, Corn

Intery, mintery, cutery, corn,

Apple seed and apple thorn;

Wire, brier, limber–lock,

Five geese in a flock,

Sit and sing by a spring,

0–u–t, and in again.

# Burnie Bee

Burnie bee, burnie bee,

Tell me when your wedding be?

If it be to-morrow day,

Take your wings and fly away.

# As I Went over Lincoln Bridge

As I went over Lincoln Bridge

I met Mister Rusticap;

Pins and needles on his back,

A–going to Thorney Fair.

# I Had a Little Hen

I had a little hen, the prettiest ever seen,

She washed me the dishes and kept the house clean;

She went to the mill to fetch me some flour,

She brought it home in less than an hour;

She baked me my bread, she

brewed me my ale,

She sat by the fire and told

many a fine tale.

# Jack Jelf

Little Jack Jelf
Was put on the shelf
Because he could not spell "pie";
When his aunt, Mrs. Grace,

Saw his sorrowful face,
She could not help saying,
"Oh, fie!"

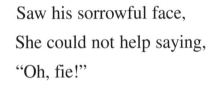

And since Master Jelf
Was put on the shelf
Because he could not
spell "pie,"

Let him stand there so grim,
And no more about him,
For I wish him a very good–bye!

# The Little Bird

Once I saw a little bird
Come hop, hop, hop;
So I cried, "Little bird,
Will you stop, stop, stop?"

I was going to the window
To say, "How do you do?"
But he shook his little tail,
And far away he flew.

# The Tailors and the Snail

Four and twenty tailors
Went to kill a snail;
The best man among them
Durst not touch her tail;
She put out her horns
Like a little Kyloe cow.
Run, tailors, run, or
She'll kill you all e'en now.

# The Man in Our Town

There was a man in our town,
And he was wondrous wise,
He jumped into a bramble bush,
And scratched out both his eyes;
But when he saw his eyes were out,
With all his might and main,
He jumped into another bush,
And scratched 'em in again.

# Winter

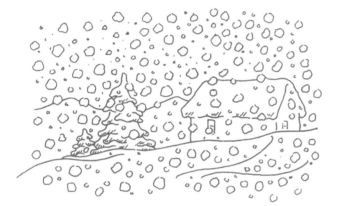

Cold and raw the north wind
doth blow,
Bleak in the morning early;
All the hills are covered with snow,
And winter's now come fairly.

# What Is the News
of the Day?

"What is the news of the day,
Good neighbor, I pray?"
"They say the balloon
Is gone up to the moon!"

# Jack–a–Nory

I'll tell you a story
About Jack–a–Nory:
And now my story's begun.
I'll tell you another
About his brother:
And now my story is done.

# Three Wise Men of Gotham

Three wise men of Gotham
Went to sea in a bowl;
If the bowl had been stronger
My song would be longer.

# Thirty White Horses

Thirty white horses upon a red hill,
Now they tramp, now they champ, now they stand still.

# Curly Locks

Curly Locks, Curly Locks, will you
    be mine?
You shall not wash dishes, nor feed
    the swine;
But sit on a cushion, and sew a
    fine seam,
And feed upon strawberries,
    sugar, and cream.

# Daffy Down Dilly

Daffy down dilly has come to town
In a yellow petticoat and a green gown.

# Shall We Go A–Shearing?

"Old woman, old woman, shall we
   go a–shearing?"
"Speak a little louder, sir, I am very
   thick of hearing."
"Old woman, old woman, shall I
   kiss you dearly?"
"Thank you, kind sir, I hear you
   very clearly."

# Friday Night's Dream

Friday night's dream, on Saturday told,
Is sure to come true, be it never so old.

# Sulky Sue

Here's Sulky Sue,
What shall we do?
Turn her face to the wall
Till she comes to.

# My Maid Mary

My maid Mary she minds the dairy
While I go a–hoeing and mowing each morn;
Gaily run the reel and the little spinning wheel.
While I am singing and mowing my corn.

# Three Children on the Ice

Three children sliding on the ice
Upon a summer's day,
As it fell out, they all fell in,
The rest they ran away.

Oh, had these children been at school,
Or sliding on dry ground,
Ten thousand dollars to
one penny
They had not then
been drowned.

So parents who have
children dear,
And you, too, who have none,
If you would keep them safe abroad
Pray keep them safe at home.

# Little Nanny Etticoat

Little Nanny Etticoat
In a white petticoat,
And a red nose;
The longer she stands
The shorter she grows.

# High In the Pine Tree

High in the pine tree,
The little turtledove
Made a little nursery
To please her little love.

"Coo," said the turtledove,
"Coo," said she;
In the long,
shady branches
Of the dark pine tree.

# Two Gray Kits

The two gray kits,
And the gray kits' mother,
All went over
The bridge together.

The bridge broke down,
They all fell in;
"May the rats go with you,"
Says Tom Bolin.

# Bedtime

The man in the moon looked out of the moon,
Looked out of the moon and said,
"'Tis time for all children on the earth
To think about getting to bed!"

# Little King Boggen

Little King Boggen, he built a fine hall,
Pie–crust and pastry–crust, that was the wall;
The windows were made of black puddings and white,
And slated with pancakes,—you ne'er saw the like!

# Leg over Leg

Leg over leg,
As the dog went to Dover;
When he came to a stile,
Jump, he went over.

# Bow Wow Wow

Bow wow wow!
Whose dog art thou?
Little Tom Tinker's dog,
Bow wow wow!

# John Smith

Is John Smith within?
Yes, that he is.
Can he set a shoe?
Ay, marry, two.
Here a nail, there a nail,
Tick, tack, too.

# Pretty John Watts

Pretty John Watts,
We are troubled with rats,
Will you drive them out of the house?
We have mice, too, in plenty,
That feast in the pantry,
But let them stay
And nibble away,
What harm in a little
brown mouse?

# Donkey, Donkey

Donkey, donkey, old and gray,
Open your mouth and gently bray;
Lift your ears and blow your horn,
To wake the world this sleepy morn.

# Bell Horses

Bell horses, bell horses,
What time of day?
One o'clock, two o'clock,
Three and away.

# Come to the Window

Come to the window,
My baby, with me,
And look at the stars
That shine on the sea!
There are two little stars
That play bo–peep
With two little fish
Far down in the deep;
And two little frogs
Cry "Neap, neap, neap";
I see a dear baby
That should be asleep.

# To Bed! To Bed!

"To bed! To bed!"
Says Sleepy–head;
"Tarry awhile," says Slow;
"Put on the pan,"
Says Greedy Nan;
"We'll sup before we go."

# We Have EVERYTHING!

OVER TWO MILLION EVERYTHING® BOOKS SOLD

Everything® **After College Book**
$12.95, 1-55850-847-3

Everything® **Angels Book**
$12.95, 1-58062-398-0

Everything® **Astrology Book**
$12.95, 1-58062-062-0

Everything® **Baby Names Book**
$12.95, 1-55850-655-1

Everything® **Baby Shower Book**
$12.95, 1-58062-305-0

Everything® **Baby's First Food Book**
$12.95, 1-58062-512-6

Everything® **Barbeque Cookbook**
$12.95, 1-58062-316-6

Everything® **Bartender's Book**
$9.95, 1-55850-536-9

Everything® **Bedtime Story Book**
$12.95, 1-58062-147-3

Everything® **Bicycle Book**
$12.00, 1-55850-706-X

Everything® **Build Your Own Home Page**
$12.95, 1-58062-339-5

Everything® **Business Planning Book**
$12.95, 1-58062-491-X

Everything® **Casino Gambling Book**
$12.95, 1-55850-762-0

Everything® **Cat Book**
$12.95, 1-55850-710-8

Everything® **Chocolate Cookbook**
$12.95, 1-58062-405-7

Everything® **Christmas Book**
$15.00, 1-55850-697-7

Everything® **Civil War Book**
$12.95, 1-58062-366-2

Everything® **College Survival Book**
$12.95, 1-55850-720-5

Everything® **Computer Book**
$12.95, 1-58062-401-4

Everything® **Cookbook**
$14.95, 1-58062-400-6

Everything® **Cover Letter Book**
$12.95, 1-58062-312-3

Everything® **Crossword and Puzzle Book**
$12.95, 1-55850-764-7

Everything® **Dating Book**
$12.95, 1-58062-185-6

Everything® **Dessert Book**
$12.95, 1-55850-717-5

Everything® **Dog Book**
$12.95, 1-58062-144-9

Everything® **Dreams Book**
$12.95, 1-55850-806-6

Everything® **Etiquette Book**
$12.95, 1-55850-807-4

Everything® **Family Tree Book**
$12.95, 1-55850-763-9

Everything® **Fly-Fishing Book**
$12.95, 1-58062-148-1

Everything® **Games Book**
$12.95, 1-55850-643-8

Everything® **Get-A-Job Book**
$12.95, 1-58062-223-2

Everything® **Get Published Book**
$12.95, 1-58062-315-8

Everything® **Get Ready for Baby Book**
$12.95, 1-55850-844-9

Everything® **Golf Book**
$12.95, 1-55850-814-7

Everything® **Guide to Las Vegas**
$12.95, 1-58062-438-3

Everything® **Guide to New York City**
$12.95, 1-58062-314-X

Everything® **Guide to Walt Disney World®, Universal Studios®, and Greater Orlando, 2nd Edition**
$12.95, 1-58062-404-9

Everything® **Guide to Washington D.C.**
$12.95, 1-58062-313-1

Everything® **Herbal Remedies Book**
$12.95, 1-58062-331-X

Everything® **Home-Based Business Book**
$12.95, 1-58062-364-6

Everything® **Homebuying Book**
$12.95, 1-58062-074-4

Everything® **Homeselling Book**
$12.95, 1-58062-304-2

Everything® **Home Improvement Book**
$12.95, 1-55850-718-3

Everything® **Hot Careers Book**
$12.95, 1-58062-486-3

Everything® **Internet Book**
$12.95, 1-58062-073-6

Everything® **Investing Book**
$12.95, 1-58062-149-X

Everything® **Jewish Wedding Book**
$12.95, 1-55850-801-5

Everything® **Job Interviews Book**
$12.95, 1-58062-493-6

Everything® **Lawn Care Book**
$12.95, 1-58062-487-1

Everything® **Leadership Book**
$12.95, 1-58062-513-4

Everything® **Low-Fat High-Flavor Cookbook**
$12.95, 1-55850-802-3

Everything® **Magic Book**
$12.95, 1-58062-418-9

Everything® **Microsoft® Word 2000 Book**
$12.95, 1-58062-306-9

# Available wherever books are sold!

Everything® **Money Book**
$12.95, 1-58062-145-7

Everything® **Mother Goose Book**
$12.95, 1-58062-490-1

Everything® **Mutual Funds Book**
$12.95, 1-58062-419-7

Everything® **One-Pot Cookbook**
$12.95, 1-58062-186-4

Everything® **Online Business Book**
$12.95, 1-58062-320-4

Everything® **Online Genealogy Book**
$12.95, 1-58062-402-2

Everything® **Online Investing Book**
$12.95, 1-58062-338-7

Everything® **Online Job Search Book**
$12.95, 1-58062-365-4

Everything® **Pasta Book**
$12.95, 1-55850-719-1

Everything® **Pregnancy Book**
$12.95, 1-58062-146-5

Everything® **Pregnancy Organizer**
$15.00, 1-58062-336-0

Everything® **Quick Meals Cookbook**
$12.95, 1-58062-488-X

Everything® **Resume Book**
$12.95, 1-58062-311-5

Everything® **Sailing Book**
$12.95, 1-58062-187-2

Everything® **Selling Book**
$12.95, 1-58062-319-0

Everything® **Study Book**
$12.95, 1-55850-615-2

Everything® **Tall Tales, Legends, and Outrageous Lies Book**
$12.95, 1-58062-514-2

Everything® **Tarot Book**
$12.95, 1-58062-191-0

Everything® **Time Management Book**
$12.95, 1-58062-492-8

Everything® **Toasts Book**
$12.95, 1-58062-189-9

Everything® **Total Fitness Book**
$12.95, 1-58062-318-2

Everything® **Trivia Book**
$12.95, 1-58062-143-0

Everything® **Tropical Fish Book**
$12.95, 1-58062-343-3

Everything® **Vitamins, Minerals, and Nutritional Supplements Book**
$12.95, 1-58062-496-0

Everything® **Wedding Book, 2nd Edition**
$12.95, 1-58062-190-2

Everything® **Wedding Checklist**
$7.95, 1-58062-456-1

Everything® **Wedding Etiquette Book**
$7.95, 1-58062-454-5

Everything® **Wedding Organizer**
$15.00, 1-55850-828-7

Everything® **Wedding Shower Book**
$7.95, 1-58062-188-0

Everything® **Wedding Vows Book**
$7.95, 1-58062-455-3

Everything® **Wine Book**
$12.95, 1-55850-808-2

---

Everything® **Angels Mini Book**
$4.95, 1-58062-387-5

Everything® **Astrology Mini Book**
$4.95, 1-58062-385-9

Everything® **Baby Names Mini Book**
$4.95, 1-58062-391-3

Everything® **Bedtime Story Mini Book**
$4.95, 1-58062-390-5

Everything® **Dreams Mini Book**
$4.95, 1-58062-386-7

Everything® **Etiquette Mini Book**
$4.95, 1-58062-499-5

Everything® **Get Ready for Baby Mini Book**
$4.95, 1-58062-389-1

Everything® **Golf Mini Book**
$4.95, 1-58062-500-2

Everything® **Love Spells Mini Book**
$4.95, 1-58062-388-3

Everything® **Pregnancy Mini Book**
$4.95, 1-58062-392-1

Everything® **TV & Movie Trivia Mini Book**
$4.95, 1-58062-497-9

Everything® **Wine Mini Book**
$4.95, 1-58062-498-7

---

Everything® **Kids' Baseball Book**
$9.95, 1-58062-489-8

Everything® **Kids' Joke Book**
$9.95, 1-58062-495-2

Everything® **Kids' Money Book**
$9.95, 1-58062-322-0

Everything® **Kids' Nature Book**
$9.95, 1-58062-321-2

Everything® **Kids' Online Book**
$9.95, 1-58062-394-8

Everything® **Kids' Puzzle Book**
$9.95, 1-58062-323-9

Everything® **Kids' Space Book**
$9.95, 1-58062-395-6

Everything® **Kids' Witches and Wizards Book**
$9.95, 1-58062-396-4

Everything® is a registered trademark of Adams Media Corporation.

**For more information, or to order, call 800-872-5627 or visit everything.com**

Adams Media Corporation, 260 Center Street, Holbrook, MA 02343

# We Have
# EVERYTHING®
# KIDS'!

Everything® Kids' Baseball Book
$9.95, 1-58062-489-8

Everything® Kids' Joke Book
$9.95, 1-58062-495-2

Everything® Kids' Money Book
$9.95, 1-58062-322-0

Everything® Kids' Nature Book
$9.95, 1-58062-321-2

Everything® Kids' Online Book
$9.95, 1-58062-394-8

Everything® Kids' Puzzle Book
$9.95, 1-58062-323-9

Everything® Kids' Space Book
$9.95, 1-58062-395-6

Everything® Kids' Witches and Wizards Book
$9.95, 1-58062-396-4

## Available wherever books are sold!

For more information, or to order,
call 800-872-5627 or visit everything.com

Adams Media Corporation, 260 Center Street, Holbrook, MA 02343

Everything® is a registered trademark of Adams Media Corporation.